The Martial Arts Book of Physics
How To Maximize Your Power, Speed, and Endurance Using The Natural Laws of Motion

by Martina Sprague

Foreword by Gene LeBell

A Division of Pro-Action Sports, Inc.

DEDICATION

To My favorite instructor Keith Livingston, for the many years of pain and glory.

ACKNOWLEDGMENT

A special thank-you to Tom, my soul mate and husband of sixteen years, who is as interested in physics as I am, and who let me bounce my ideas off of him. Also, thank-you to my martial arts students who have provided me with so many opportunities to think about and analyze techniques and concepts. And, finally, thank-you to Ake Johansson, my first physics instructor in Sweden. It was he who was instrumental in helping me develop a love for physics, and who sparked my interest from the beginning by asking; "Why is the forest, when seen through a glass of water, upside down?"

Editor: Stuart Sobel
Assistant Editor: Felipe Flores-Islas
Graphic Design: Mit Design
Front Cover Design Artist: Steve Kim
Cover Design Concept: Stuart Sobel
Photos: They are either from the archives of Pro-Action Publishing or have the by line of Thomas Sprague or Martina Sprague. The photos are noted as to its origin in the body of the book.
Assisting Martina Sprague in the photo techniques are Keith Livingston and Mark Livingston.

Printed in the United States of America
ISBN No. 1-890378-01-1
Library of Congress No. 00 090835

GENE LEBELL FOREWORD

Many people have called me, "the toughest man alive". I never gave myself that title, but I have to admit that there was never anyone I didn't think I could beat, once I could pounce on my older brother. But if someone said the word "physics" to me in high school, that would definitely scare me. I would avoid physics like it was the class bully and I was the class wimp.

When I first began to study the combative arts I actually had a better advantage than your average student because I began with the best in the world. You see, my parents ran the world famous Olympic Auditorium in Los Angeles. Mom (Aileen Eaton) was, for almost 40 years, the world's only major female boxing promoter. To date no one has been able to fill her shoes. When she retired she became the head of the State Athletic Commission for California. My step-dad Cal Eaton, and my brother Mike were in charge of the pro-wrestling and roller derby for the arena. As for me, all I ever wanted to do was compete. I had no interest in the business end of the business. I was only interested in applying the business end of a finishing hold.

When I was in school, little did it ever occur to me to go to a physics professor to find out how to perfect my martial arts techniques. Believe it or not, my first instructor, a champion pro-wrestler by the name of Ed "Strangler" Lewis never once said to me, "Learn the laws of physics boy, it you want to be really great". If he had, I would have learned this subject without a question.

My mom knew that I was no scholar, so it never dawned on her to have me go to a physics camp over the summer. It never popped into my head that techniques could be diagrammed as a formula before I ever stepped foot onto the mat. I knew what felt right and how I could generate the most power. I had no idea that I was actually applying natural laws. As far as I was concerned, it was just trial and error until I got a move correct.

Applying the laws of physics not only demonstrated to me how I should position myself for an ideal advantage, but it also pointed the way on how to maneuver my opponent to his disadvantage. The natural laws of motion are the same whether you are bigger or smaller than your opponent. If these physics equations are applied properly, the outcome will be consistent.

With well over 50 years of involvement in the martial arts I thought I've seen every conceivable way to teach this subject. I have to admit though, THE MARTIAL ARTS BOOK OF PHYSICS is a new one on me. You can apply this to all of the styles and systems of the martial arts. This is without a doubt practical, and a most enjoyable way to learn this facet of physics. As for the author Martina Sprague, to be able to explain both subjects with such proficiency is a credit to her own dedication.

What's more, The Martial Arts Book of Physics is presented in a most logical and constructive manner. Each physics term is defined in the chapter and then placed in a glossary as the end of that chapter. Also, look at the end of the chapter. Do not pass up the quiz section. In addition, you will find many of your favorite martial art pioneers and champions practicing techniques, while all the time not being aware that they are using the laws of physics correctly.

Physics is not as scary to me as I had once had thought. Nor would I shy away from discussing it. Look at me, talking about physics. Who would have believed it. All I can say is , Mom would have been proud". And if your instructor hasn't told you already, let me be the first, "Learn the laws of physics, if you want to be really great".

Keep smiling
Gene LeBell

COMMENTS FROM THE PUBLISHER

This is a most extraordinary book. I've been involved in the martial arts for over 25 years and have seen the availability of martial arts books grow to the vast array that is now available around the world. I've even helped in adding to that number. However, of the massive number of books that I've seen, I have never seen a book that had mixed martial arts and physics. It's a natural combination. But I'll start at the beginning.

The manuscript was sent unsolicited over a year ago. We make it a standing rule to examine everything that comes in. If it doesn't grab and hold our interest within the first few pages, it won't hold our readers interest either and we toss it unless otherwise requested. However, this was not the case in The Martial Arts Book of Physics. I couldn't put it down. It then went to the manager of Pro-Action, Felipe Flores. He too was intrigued and also couldn't put it down. Martina Sprague broke our long standing rule, which made me think of that James Bond film, Never Say Never. Our long standing rule is that we do not publish anyone that either doesn't have a world class name and reputation and/or is recognized as an authority in their field.

I personally spoke with Martina, offered suggestions in expanding this project and then, the race was on. The topic of martial arts was expanded to include all of the arts, not just the arts in the treatment. What do you know, the principles of physics applies to all of them. I also wanted to know about the laws of physics that govern demonstrations. Bruce Lee's one inch punch was one of them.

What I discovered was that in demos, including the infamous One Inch Punch, physics held the key. This is not to say that knowing the laws of physics is all you have to know. What it means is that it takes incredible strength, timing and focus, ie. chi perfomed with precision in order to be successful. So it is true, in order to apply the laws of physics as prescribed you must have "chi". That only proves the masters were correct with their instruction all along.

After being involved with the martial arts for as long as I have, I can tell if someone knows what they are talking about the arts. However, with physics, well that's a different story. What the author said regarding martial arts was correct. Her experience as an instructor and competitor was on the mark. What she said regarding physics sounded logical, but I just didn't know. So, I went to those that did know. One professor from UCLA and the other from Santa Monica College were both kind enough to go through the manuscript for me to verify that all of the physics were correct. She did know her physics as well as her martial arts. One of the professors even thought this might be an excellent book to introduce the beginning student to physics.

In order to make the learning process easier, Martina Sprague has created a quiz after each chapter. There is even a glossary of physics terms after each chapter as well. You will find that some of these terms are duplicated in several chapters. This was done on purpose so you wouln't have to remember which chapter you first saw the word and it's definition. You just look at the end of the chapter to the Glossary.

A note of caution. Like anything new that you will ever learn, you have to work at it to make it yours. Everyone progresses at their own level, but once you truly understand it, your performance will soar. I guarantee it.

Stuart Sobel

MARTINA SPRAGUE BIOGRAPHY

Martina grew up in Stockholm, Sweden. She has always had an interest in aviation, and her goal initially was to become a professional pilot. She begin flying sail planes when she was only fifteen years of age. The following year she got her license for power planes. She actually knew how to fly four years before she learned how to drive a car. It was during these early years in Stockholm that she was introduced to the world of physics.

At seventeen she came to America as an exchange student, ending up at Indianapolis, Indiana. It was during this time that she met, and four years later married, her husband Tom. The two moved to Salt Lake City, Utah where Martina graduated from Westminster College with a Bachelor of Science Degree in Aviation (professional pilot emphasis). Her plan was to go into astrophysics and work for NASA. Cut-backs in funding made it impossible for her to follow that goal.

After graduating from college she began to work for Delta Air Lines, being responsible for calculating weight loads by balancing the cargo for each aircraft. In addition, she also became a flight instructor.

At age of 23 years she entered a dojo for the first time. The system was aikido. Her knowledge of physics, which she studied throughout her educational career, became extremely useful. Much to her surprise though, the art was not physical enough for her.

Her next stop was at Ed Parker's kenpo karate. She studied this system for almost four years, entering every tournament she could. Then, the final stop, kick-boxing.

At 28 she walked into South Salt Lake City police officer Keith Livingston's kick-boxing academy. The reality check was about to take place. Taking more lumps and bumps than she ever had in the past, Martina kept coming back for more, dishing it out as she was taking it. She advanced as she always had, in a rapid manner. She tested the theory that she learned in three amateur kick-boxing bouts. She eventually became an instructor at the Livingston school.

In all of her many careers and hobbies, whether it was avionics or martial arts, her knowledge and passion for physics gave her the decided edge. Translated, physics can apply to any physical thing that you do in a most meaningful, and profound way. Her view is from both sides of the ropes. She has a working knowledge as a proficient instructor in both traditional and full-contact karate and has also been a competitor in both. Add to that her understanding of the natural laws of motion, and all I can say is, "watch out." Martina displays a passion and a winner's attitude for everything she tries. Who knew that her love of physics and her love of the martial arts would finally converge. Knowing how organized Martina is, I'm sure it was all a part of her master plan all along.

Table Of Contents

Preface

You hate physics? You're just not a math whiz? Many people squirm when they hear the word"physics", and the first thing that comes to mind are numbers and letters mixed into some sort of incomprehensible language called equations. Well, don't worry! The physics that we will be discussing in this book is "conceptual physics", which relies mainly on concepts rather than equations. Concepts are ideas that the reader is already familiar with. These ideas are then related to martial arts (power, in particular). The following equations, which you will see in the text, are there only to strengthen the concepts.

1. Momentum = mass (weight) X velocity (speed)
2. Force = mass X acceleration
3. Torque = lever arm X force
4. Impulse = force X time
5. Work = force X distance
6. Power = work/time
7. Kinetic energy = 1/2 mass X velocity squared

The equations will be embedded in the text and where appropriate, will appear inside of a box above a picture relating to the equation. The equations will also use different size lettering to show which component part of the equation is strongest, as shown below:

Change in momentum = force x time
or
Impulse = Ft

Impulse=Ft   Impulse=Ft

In the equation Impulse = Ft, a small size F indicates a small force, and a large size t indicates a longtime (left picture), whereas a large size F indicates a large force, and a small size t indicates a short time (right picture). This will help the reader visualize what is happening both through the pictures and text, through the equation in the box, and through the different size lettering in the equation above the picture.

Note: Different size lettering is not the same as upper or lower case, and is used only to emphasize which part of the equation that is most significant to power. F will always be upper case, and t will always be lower case, simply because that's how it is written for consistency in the world of physics.

As you study this book, you will find that certain words that have an exact meaning in physics have occasionally been used in a more everyday type of language. An example would be the word "power". In physics, power is defined as work/time. To the martial artist however, power takes on a different meaning, and is commonly used to determine how much damage one is able to do when landing a strike. The way the martial artist uses the word "power" might be disturbing to the student of physics. It should be borne in mind however, that the book is written primarily for the student of martial arts. For the purpose of this book, "power" explained later, should be thought of as the force of impact of a punch or kick. "Power" has also been described as a vector, but for this to be true in physics, it would be more appropriate to substitute "power" with "force". A student of physics might also frown on the fact that I have used numbers only in most of the equations, without specifying the units.This has been done for simplification purposes, as the book focuses on concepts rather than equations. To tell a martial arts student that he should strike with a force of a certain number of newtons, would have meaning only if he had some prior knowledge of physics.

I am confident that you will find the concepts of physics and martial arts discussed in this book enjoyable and easy to understand.

Introduction

I once knew a martial artist who claimed that his instructor had such terrific powers that he could strike you from across the room without being within reach to physically touch you. I had at that time studied martial arts on a daily basis for about seven years, and being a down to earth type of person, this martial artist's claim did not only seem ridiculous; it did not even raise an ounce of curiosity in me. We have all heard stories of such feats a hundred times, but we have yet to meet the person who can support them. Because I respected this martial artist as a good person and excellent sparring partner, I let the issue go and did not comment on it further. But as the years went by, I was wondering what had made him and so many others in the martial arts support this "mind over matter" type of fighting. After giving the issue substantial thought, and after disregarding possible differences in semantics, I found that it is in fact:

- Possible to strike a person from a distance without physically touching him, but only if that person knows in advance that he is going to get hit.

- Not possible to strike a person from a distance without physically touching him, if that person uses his own "powers" to counteract the blow.

And then there are those martial artists who walk barefoot on burning coal. Although to the onlookers it takes a certain amount of fortitude to perform the feat, I am not sure what exactly this is supposed to prove as far as martial arts is concerned. Intellectually however, I understand the principles of physics behind these claims and others. Read on, and I will reveal the "secrets". Martial arts means the intricate study of combat. The purpose of this book is to analyze, according to the principles of physics, one of the most important assets to successful fighting: power. It has been said that to be a successful martial artist, you don't need size or strength, because "it is all in the technique". It has also been said that the power of a martial artist seems to increase quickly with weight, and that the best lightweight fighter in the world will be defeated every time by an unranked heavyweight in a bar brawl.

So, which is it? Is it your size and physical strength that makes you the winner, or is it your experience and dedication to correct technique?

Most books about power in the martial arts rely heavily on physical conditioning and prompt the reader to do push-ups and sit-ups and plyometrics exercise in explosive power. I will attempt to take you through the "back door" and show you the principles of physics behind power. My purpose is not to negate the importance of physical conditioning, but rather to complement it by broadening your understanding of the laws of nature, the importance of correct technique, and how a smaller person can indeed make these laws work to his advantage.

Let me take you on the power trip, and I will show you the easy way how $F = ma$.

CHAPTER 1
Center Of Gravity

Balance, How Important Is It?

When looking back, I consider my karate training much more ritualized than the kick-boxing training I later received. From the beginning, students were expected to do things a certain way, and if deviating from this pattern we might suddenly find ourselves on the floor without really knowing how we got there. Certain rituals had to be adhered to; bowing when stepping into the dojo, lining up according to our rank, and keeping a strong focus on the instructor and the techniques taught. After warm-up and stretching, we often started with drills in the basic punches and kicks. This was always done from a horse stance, so called because of its similarity to a person riding on a horse.

Men riding on horses.

Fighters in horse stances.

(From the archives of Pro-Action Publishing)

We were told to keep our feet about shoulder width and a half apart, with our knees slightly bent. The instructor would then call out the punches and we would follow with a loud kiai. If the classes were large, there were often one or more assistant instructors present, who would walk between the rows of students. Every so often, I would see, from the corner of my eye, a student in an adjacent row tumble to the floor. The instructor had swept the student's foot, taking him off balance. Every time the instructor neared me, I feared I would get swept. This was not a malicious move on the part of the instructor, but simply an attempt to make us understand the importance of balance and correct posture.

In addition to strengthening the legs, the horse stance serves the purpose of stability. In general, when we talk about physical stability, we mean an object or person who possesses balance and will not tip over easily. Judo players and grapplers, for example, need a great deal of balance to counteract their opponent's tries to throw them to the ground.

Sumo wrestlers manipulating balance.
(From the archives of Pro-Action Publishing)

Stand-up fighters also need balance in order to deliver a strike or kick with maximum power.
(From the archives of Pro-Action Publishing)

Because successful fighting depends on gaining a positional advantage, a fighter is seldom tied to one spot. It now becomes necessary to learn all over again how to "walk". Moving from one spot to another when fighting is not as simple as taking a step forward. Many factors need to be considered; among those are superior positioning and balance. This led to the development of the Basic Movement Theory, which states that whenever moving, you should step with the foot closest to the direction of travel first. For example, to move forward, you should step with your lead foot first and readjust the width of your stance with your rear foot. To move backward, you should step with your rear foot first and readjust the width of your stance with your lead foot. The primary reason for the development of the Basic Movement Theory is to keep a fighter from crossing his feet.

Which fighter appears to be in the more stable stance, Andrew Linick (L) or Benny Urquidez? Why is the horse stance more stable than a stance in which your feet are close together or crossed?
(From the archives of Pro-Action Publishing, photo on right by Stuart Sobel)

Center Of Gravity

A few years later when I became an instructor myself, I loved the push-up routine. Schools of self-defense often advertise that "you don't need size and strength to defend yourself effectively against a bigger opponent". Being the skeptical person I was, I insisted upon my students developing strength. We would do ten push-ups, and then I would ask them to hold the down position without touching the floor with any body part other than the hands and feet. When they were nearly blue in the face, I would check their geography knowledge:

**What's the capital of Madagascar?
Tanana . . .what?!
Spell it!**

When doing more research into push-ups I found that, because you lift such a small percentage of your body weight, the "girl push-up" (on your knees) is nearly useless for developing upper body strength. I also found that when doing a regular push-up, men lift slightly more of their body weight than do women. Why is that? I used to tell my students that it is because women have bigger butts (because I am a woman, I felt it was safe to say this). In relation to overall body structure, the average man is more top heavy than the average woman. But is the bigger butt necessarily such a bad thing? It all depends on what you're trying to achieve. Whether the glass is half-full or half-empty depends on what's in the glass, and how desirable that substance is to the person who has to drink it. I found that being bottom heavy is advantageous to the martial artist.

Oh, by the way, Madagascar is a large island east of the south tip of Africa. The capital of Madagascar is Antananarivo.

Center of gravity (or center of mass) refers to the point on any object where all its weight seems to be focused. We can also think of center of gravity as the balance point. If you take an object of uniform shape and weight, its balance point is its center. If you take an object of non-uniform shape and weight, its balance point will be toward the heavier end. Assuming that the weight per square inch is equal throughout the following objects, where will you find each object's center of gravity?

A pyramid has a low center of gravity and is very stable because of its wide base. The wider the base, and the more weight that is concentrated in the base, the more stable the object will be. For maximum stability, you would therefore keep a stance that is as low and wide as possible. There is, however, a trade-off. If your stance gets too wide, you will sacrifice mobility for stability. If fighting relied on stability only, you would study such arts that employ a very low and wide stance. But since force is a combination of mass and acceleration, which in turn branch off into many other different components, fighting becomes a "give and take" situation, where sometimes you will need to make a sacrifice in one area in order to gain an advantage in another.

Now take a look a the following two pyramids. Which one is more stable?

In both cases, the base is wider than the top. But in relation to its own height, the pyramid on the left has a wider base than the pyramid on the right. Let's look at what exactly it is that makes the pyramid on the left the most stable of the two.

Stability depends on two factors:

- How high you need to raise the center of gravity in order to make the object "top heavy". The wider the base, the higher the center of gravity must be raised before the object will tip over.

- If you drop a line straight down from the center of gravity of an object of any shape, and it falls within the foundation of that object, the object is stable. If it falls outside of the foundation, the object is unstable.

I'm sure you can see just by looking at these objects that quite an effort would be required to tip the left pyramid on its side. In the right pyramid, the center of gravity is already quite high, so this pyramid will be easier to tip over.

In addition to being more stable, the pyramid on the left has its weight focused over a larger surface area than the pyramid on the right. This principle of pounds per square inch can be applied to finger push-ups. Because the fingers are inherently weak and must support the full weight of the body, finger push-ups take a great deal of strength. The more you can spread your weight, however, the easier the push-up will be. When starting to train in finger push-ups, you should therefore keep both your hands and feet wide apart. This will spread your weight over a large surface area with less force per square inch. The two-finger handstand that master Mas Oyama demonstrates in the picture below takes both strength and balance, but would be even more difficult if his hands were closer together. Notice also how his body is pyramid shaped for greater stability.

Mas Oyama demonstrates a two-finger handstand.
(From the archives of Pro-Action Publishing)

If you are a grappler, you will find that less effort is needed to pin your opponent to the ground if you stay as low as possible. Spreading your weight and staying low (wide base, low center of gravity) will make it very difficult for your opponent to throw you off, even if he possesses size and strength. Standing on your opponent and keeping an upright posture (narrow base, high center of gravity) will make it easier for your opponent to throw you off.

In both cases below, the fighter on the bottom is in the prone position face down. Would you say that he has a good chance of winning this fight? Well, it depends a lot on how stable the fighter on top is. If you were the fighter on the bottom, who would you rather deal with: a bottom heavy or a top heavy opponent?

Wide base, low center of gravity.
(stable)

(From the archives of Pro-Action Publishing)

Narrower base, higher center of gravity.
(not as stable)

(From the archives of Pro-Action Publishing)

The second factor that determines stability is whether a line dropped straight down from the center of gravity falls within the foundation of the object. This concept becomes especially important whenever we throw a kick with our lead leg, as we shall soon see.

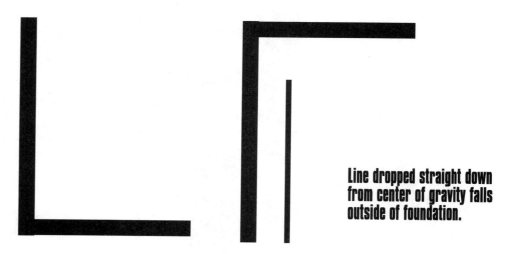

Line dropped straight down from center of gravity falls outside of foundation.

Of these two objects, the one on the left is more stable than the one on the right, not only because it has a wider base, but also because a line dropped straight down from the center of gravity will fall within the base of the object. The object on the right, however, is lopsided and will tip over.

This gymnast is in a balanced state because her center of gravity is directly above the narrow base of her hands. The karate practitioner performing a side thrust kick is also in a balanced state because his center of gravity falls directly above the narrow base of his foot. If the karate practitioner's upper body wasn't angled backwards in the opposite direction of the kick, he would be unable to maintain balance. Try it!

The reverse handstand seen in the picture below is an exercise in balance more than in strength. Because the hands (the foundation) are closer to the head than to the feet, in order to perform a handstand at a diagonal angle, the hands must be reversed. If the fingers were pointing towards the head instead, the foundation would shift horizontally closer to the head, the center of gravity would not fall above the foundation, and maintaining balance at this angle would not be possible.

Hidy Ochiai performs a reverse handstand.
(From the archives of Pro-Action Publishing, photo by Tom Decker)

Balance Manipulation In Throws

Successful throws rely on your ability to manipulate your opponent's balance. Judo is well known for its dynamic throws. When two people are tied together, as is the case when one person is throwing another, an interesting thing occurs: In regard to balance, the two fighters will begin to act as one. Physics does not know that the two fighters are separate entities. With this in mind, ask yourself what the objective of the throw is and where the center of gravity is located.

The objective of a judo throw is to get your opponent on the ground, but without going down with him. If you grab your opponent and hoist him over your shoulder in preparation for a throw, your feet are the only foundation, but both your bodies joined together will determine where the center of gravity is. The picture below is an example of how the combined center of gravity for these two fighters falls outside of the foundation. The throw is therefore not successful. The fighter executing the throw will go down with his opponent.

The center of gravity falls outside of the foundation.
The person executing the throw will go down with his opponent.
[From the archives of Pro-Action Publishing]

Before a successful throw can come to completion, it requires a balanced state of the two bodies. The next picture is an example of this balanced state at the initiation of a throw. Note how the combined center of gravity is above the very small foundation of the thrower's left foot. Because the person initiating the throw has maintained balance between the two bodies, the next step, the throw itself, will have a potentially successful outcome.

Balanced state at the initiation of a throw.
(From the archives of Pro-Action Publishing)

The final phase of the throwing stage relies on the principle of making your opponent's center of gravity only fall outside of the foundation, while your own center of gravity remains above the foundation. As you can see in the next picture, the foundation is the distance between the thrower's two feet. The thrower's body is nearly upright with the center of gravity above the foundation. The center of gravity of the person being thrown, however, falls outside of the thrower's foundation. Because the two bodies act as a unit, when the thrower begins to feel the effects of the throw, he must "let" his opponent fall. If he persists in holding onto his opponent tightly, the two bodies will continue to act as one, their combined center of gravity will not be above the foundation, and the thrower will go down with his opponent.

Correct mechanics, and full understanding of center of gravity, enables a lighter and weaker person to throw a heavier and stronger opponent. In the picture below the opponent is in the vertical upside down position, with his feet almost touching the ceiling. Yet, very little energy is required to execute the throw.

Note also how the thrower's right arm is extended backward to shift the center of gravity slightly to the rear. This will help him maintain balance.

Successful throw with full control of balance.
(From the archives of Pro-Action Publishing)

Once your opponent starts going over your hip, his center of gravity will fall outside of his foundation and will begin to act to your advantage. As long as your body mechanics are correct with your own balance maintained, the rest of the throw will happen almost automatically. A 100 pound girl, who has received the appropriate training, can with ease throw a 200 pound man in this way.

Balance Manipulation In Joint Locks And Other Takedowns

One of the easiest ways for a smaller person to defeat a bigger adversary is by attacking the inherently weak areas. It doesn't matter how big or muscular your opponent is, he cannot flex his eyeballs, ear drums, or testicles. However, getting to a position from where you can easily use a strike against these targets is a different matter. If you can get your opponent on the ground without going down with him, you have a distinct advantage. You have now bought time which may allow you to escape, while your opponent must expend energy defeating the forces of gravity and inertia to get back on his feet. Balance manipulation is one of the easiest ways to get your opponent on the ground. In addition, since the neck is an inherently weak area with a high center of gravity, if you can use the neck to shift your opponent's balance, not much physical strength is needed to take a bigger adversary down.

Grappling master Gene LeBell uses neck manipulation in conjunction with a joint lock to shift his opponent's center of gravity.
(From the archives of Pro-Action Publishing)

In a grappling situation, the closer your technique is to your own center of mass, the more strength you will appear to have. If you were to lift a 100 pound box, would it be easier to lift it with your arms extended and the weight away from your body, or with your arms bent and the weight as close to your body as possible? The latter is true, because keeping the weight close to your body allows you to use the strength of your entire body to produce the force, and not just the muscular strength in your arms.

The same concept is true for takedowns. Keeping the technique close to your center of mass allows you to use your body weight and not your muscular strength. Most takedowns also rely on circular motion. You will conserve energy by keeping the technique close to the center of the circle. Very little movement is now needed on your part, while a lot of movement is needed for your opponent.

In the picture below, Gene LeBell is utilizing two principles of physics: First, he is pulling his opponent forward and off balance, relying on his opponent's forward momentum. Second, he can now execute a joint lock against the wrist followed by a takedown, using very little strength because the technique is so close to his own center of mass.

Gene LeBell pulls his opponent off balance and close to his own center of mass.
(From the archives of Pro-Action Publishing)

In any throw, takedown, or lock-up, if you can shift your opponent's center of gravity so that it is no longer above the foundation, the takedown is not only probable; it is certain. In the picture below, world champion kick-boxer Benny "The Jet" Urquidez is immobilizing his opponent's arm to keep him from regaining balance. "The Jet" then pushes his opponent's upper body to the rear, until the center of gravity (the balance point) has shifted so much that it is no longer above the foundation. His opponent will lose balance backwards.

World champion kick-boxer Benny "The Jet" manipulates his opponent's balance by shifting the center of gravity.
(From the archives of Pro-Action Publishing)

Balance In The Hard And Soft Styles

How balance is maintained is also reflected in the many different styles of karate. Karate is divided into "hard" and "soft" styles. Somebody not educated on the subject might assume that hard and soft refer to the effectiveness of the style, or how painful the techniques might be. That is not the case. The hard styles (in general the Japanese styles) utilize wide stances and linear moves, whereas the soft styles (in general the Chinese styles) utilize more flexibility in their stances and circular moves. There is also a wide variety of styles that fall in between these extremes.

Practitioners of Shotokan karate, one of the hardest of the hard styles, rely on wide stances to maintain balance. The picture below shows Italian karate champion Falsoni demonstrating a linear strike from the Shotokan style.

(From the archives of Pro-Action Publishing)

The soft style of Kung-Fu, on the other hand, utilizes the movement of the body to maintain balance. This is similar in concept to the way a chicken or pigeon maintains balance; the head has to move forward or back each time a step is taken. In the pictures below, the Kung-Fu practitioner moves his body in the opposite direction of his arms. Note also how the strikes are circular in nature.

(From the archives of Pro-Action Publishing)

The hard styles rely on the "one-strike" concept, with maximum power in the linear direction. These linear strikes usually start from long range, allowing the practitioner to build momentum through forward movement. The linear strike is economical in time (the shortest distance between two points is a straight line) and usually focuses on the opponent's centerline, where some of the most vulnerable targets are located. Hard strikes are great for catching an aggressive opponent off balance, especially if such fighter is in the process of throwing a kick.

As demonstrated by Numano's punch against Louis Delgado, when combined with forward momentum, the linear "hard strike" is great for stealing balance.
(From the archives of Pro-Action Publishing)

The linear strike can be likened to a block (as opposed to a parry) that meets power with power. When your opponent is stopped in his tracks, he will experience a jarring effect that will set him back, push him off balance, and force him to regroup.

The drawback of the hard style "one-strike" concept is that all energy is focused into that one strike, and if the strike fails to do the intended damage, it will take both energy and speed to reposition for a follow-up technique.

The soft styles, on the other hand, give the practitioner a bit more versatility. Soft arts rely on circular motion with strikes in combinations, where the "finishing" strike builds speed for power through one or more "set-up" strikes. This circular motion allows the practitioner to build tremendous momentum, and to work at close range from a superior position around his opponent's back. Multiple strikes in combinations also tend to split your opponent's focus and cause sensory overload.

Mas Oyama's circular "soft strikes" work well from a side or rear position in close quarters.
(From the archives of Pro-Action Publishing)

In principle, a soft strike can be likened to a parry. The idea is to keep your opponent's motion going, thereby unbalancing him and drawing him into a follow-up strike. Soft styles are yielding, using your opponent's own energy against himself.

We, as fighters, have a natural tendency to focus our attacks straight ahead, but there are many advantages to working the angled attacks of the soft styles. When going directly against the force, balance can only be manipulated if your opponent already has a narrow base. This is also why the sideways fighting stance is so beneficial in the frontal direction where most attacks are aimed; you can brace yourself with your rear leg. The soft styles, on the other hand, allow you superiority to the side or back of your opponent's body, allowing you to attack at an angle away from his focused power.

As shown by Bill Wallace (L) and Joe Lewis, balance, in the soft styles, can be manipulated by aiming the attack at a target that is naturally weak.
(From the archives of Pro-Action Publishing, photo by Mary Townsley)

The Power Of The Lead Leg Kick

When I was studying karate, I used the lead leg front kick a lot, because it was fast and easy to throw, and could often score a point against an opponent with ease. When I started in kick-boxing several years later, my instructor told me that my lead leg front kick was lousy and totally lacked power, and that his grandma, who was 85 years old and had had hip surgery, had a stronger kick than mine.

Man, your kicks are lousy! You ain't scaring this old lady!

I went home and practiced on the heavy bag, and discovered that the rear leg front kick was slower, but much more powerful than the lead. I also found that my lead foot was often slightly short of reaching its target, or that the foot was sliding against the heavy bag instead of kicking into it. Because competition kick-boxing relies on powerful strikes and kicks more so than competition in a traditional martial art, in which the fighter relies on scoring points instead of knocking his opponent out, the question now became whether I should abandon the lead leg kick and throw all of my front kicks with the rear leg. But because the lead leg is so quick, I didn't want to give it up, and so I began to research the reason behind the lesser power of the lead leg.

To maintain balance when throwing a kick, you must do one of the following:

- Center your upper body (center of gravity) above your supporting foot (base).
- Center your supporting foot (base) underneath your upper body (center of gravity).

If you fail to do this, your center of gravity will not be above your foundation, and you will lose balance. And why is this important to power, and especially so when throwing a kick with your lead leg? Let me ask you this: Do you agree that a front kick or round house kick thrown with your lead leg is generally less powerful than the same kick thrown with your rear leg? To some people the power of the lead leg is a flexibility issue, but assuming that you have good flexibility in both legs, the lead leg is less powerful because:

- The distance between the lead leg and the target is shorter than the distance between the rear leg and the target. The shorter the distance, the less time is available to build momentum for power. We will talk about this in more detail later.

- The center of gravity (your upper body) must be above your supporting foot (in this case, your rear foot).

Note how Benny "The Jet's" center of gravity is located in his upper body, aft lead foot and forward of his rear.

When "The Jet" raises his lead foot, he must center his upper body above his supporting rear foot.

When "The Jet" extends his lead leg to kick, his upper body moves an additional few inches to the rear for balance.
(From the archives of Pro-Action Publishing)

    Because the center of gravity and the foundation must be vertically lined up for balance, as your lead foot comes off the floor to throw the kick, you must move your upper body slightly to the rear until it is centered above your rear foot. The drawback of this is that your upper body will move in the opposite direction of the kick, causing opposing movement and splitting the power into two different directions (most of it forward, but some of it back). The remedy for this then, is to move your rear foot forward and underneath your upper body instead of moving your upper body back and above your rear foot. This can be accomplished by taking a small step forward with your rear foot prior to throwing the kick.

Note how Benny "The Jet" steps forward with his rear foot until it is centered underneath his upper body. When he has achieved balance, he throws the lead leg front kick.
(From the archives of Pro-Action Publishing)

So, what's the trade-off? Well, whenever you step prior to throwing a kick, you will add movement and the time it takes to step, and will therefore run the risk of telegraphing the kick. Stepping with your rear foot will also narrow your stance for a short time, which defies the Basic Movement Theory. To throw a powerful lead leg kick, you must make a sacrifice in another area: movement and time.

Note: When throwing a front kick or round house kick with the rear leg, your upper body will automatically move forward above your supporting lead foot. A step prior to throwing a kick with your rear leg is therefore not required, and the forward movement of your upper body will add additional power to the kick.

Balance Quiz

1.   What are the advantages of the horse stance? Disadvantages?

Because of its wide base and low center of gravity, the horse stance is a very stable stance. In addition, it allows you full focus on your hand techniques when practicing. But because the horse stance is somewhat rigid and wide, it limits your mobility. All targets on your centerline will also be exposed to your opponent's strikes. The horse stance is therefore used more as a training stance than a fighting stance.

2.   How can you increase stability when in a stand-up type fight? When in a ground fight?

You can always increase stability by widening your base and lowering your center of gravity. If in a stand-up type fight, bend your knees. If in a ground fight, spread out.

3.   If in a left fighting stance (left foot forward), when circling your opponent, which foot should you step with first and why?

When circling left, step with your lead foot first; when circling right, step with your rear foot first. This will keep you from narrowing your stance or crossing your feet, which is destructive to balance.

4.   How do you keep from squaring your stance when circling an opponent? Why is it important to keep a sideways stance?

In order to maintain a sideways stance when circling, your rear foot must take a bigger step than your lead foot. This is because your rear foot is farther from the center of the circle. If circling right from a left fighting stance, and your steps are equal, you will eventually end up in a crossed stance. If the step with your rear foot is too big however, you will eventually end up in a square stance. A square stance will expose your centerline and make you unable to keep the full weight of your body behind your strikes, which in turn will lessen power.

5.   Why is the "girl push-up" nearly useless for building upper body strength?

The farther the weight is from the pivotal point, the more strength is required to lift it. When doing push-ups on your knees, the pivotal point (your knees) is much closer to the weight (your upper body) than when doing push-ups on your toes. As a result, you lift only half or less of your body weight. The regular push-up enables you to lift about 75 percent of your body weight.

6.   Where is the center of gravity located on a horse shoe shaped object?

The center of gravity is always located toward the heavier end. On a horse shoe shaped object, the center of gravity is located in the open space toward the closed end of the arc. The center of gravity does not have to fall within the tangible parts of the object, only within the center of mass.

7.   Why is the fighter throwing the side thrust kick able to maintain balance, even though his base is very narrow and his center of gravity quite high?

Because the fighter's upper body is angled to the rear, his center of gravity is directly above his foundation (supporting foot). He is therefore in a balanced state. Any time you kick, you must center your upper body above your foundation.

8   Why is a punch or kick thrown with your lead hand (foot) naturally less powerful than the same strike thrown with your rear hand (foot)? Are there any advantages to throwing strikes with your lead hand (foot)?

Lead strikes have less distance available to build momentum for power. The advantage of the lead strike is that it is often faster than the rear, and therefore not telegraphed as easily.

9.   How do you remedy the lesser power of the lead strike?

The power of the lead strike can be increased by taking a step forward. This will add momentum and the weight of your body to the strike.

Glossary

Balance–When the center of gravity falls above the foundation, an object is in a stable state and will not tip over easily.

Basic Movement Theory--Whenever moving, you should step with the foot closest to the direction of travel first. This will keep you from crossing your feet and becoming unstable. Stepping with the foot closest to the direction of travel first will also allow for smoother and quicker movement.

Center Of Gravity (same as center of mass)–The point on an object where all its weight seems to be focused. On an object of uniform shape and weight, the center of gravity is in the middle. On an object of non-uniform shape and weight, the center of gravity is toward the heavier end. To remain stable, the center of gravity should be as low as possible, and above the foundation.

Gravity–An attraction between objects due to mass.

Hard Styles–These styles rely on wide stances and linear moves, with full focus of power into a single strike.

Horse Stance–A training stance simulating a person riding on a horse. The horse stance is used mostly for practicing basic striking, allowing you to focus on your hand techniques. It also strengthens your legs and helps you maintain balance. When engaged in actual sparring, a fighter should use a modified horse stance that is not as rigid, but in which his knees are still bent, and his feet are still about shoulder width and a half apart.

Inertia–Resistance to change in motion. An object at rest tends to stay at rest; an object in motion tends to stay in motion.

Mass–The quantity of matter in an object. When acted upon by gravity, we can use mass interchangeably with weight.

Momentum–The product of the mass of an object and its velocity. The heavier the object, and the faster it travels, the greater the momentum.

Pounds Per Square Inch–The narrower the base of an object, the more pounds per square inch. A narrow base will be less stable than a wide base, but it will also have more penetrating capability.

Sensory Overload–By striking and kicking with explosive combinations to as many targets as possible in the shortest amount of time, you will create "sensory overload" and send your opponent into a state of confusion and chaos.

Soft Styles–These styles rely on more flexible stances and circular moves, with the power building through one or more "set-up" strikes.

CHAPTER 2
Momentum

Without Movement, Nothing Happens

When I awoke this morning, I felt as though I had been sleeping on rocks. I tried to remember whether I had taken a lot of kicks to the ribs the previous day. Then I remembered that I had grappled with my instructor, who weighs 200 pounds. Because I only weigh 120 pounds, for the majority of the time I had been on the bottom, trying to keep this enormous mountain of mass from squashing me into the floor. When I finally tapped out because I couldn't breathe, my instructor told me that to defeat him I must rely on speed and explosiveness, which in turn would enable me to work into a better position, from where I could then attack his weaker areas.

We started the grappling from a stand-up position. In order to grapple, you must first close in on your opponent. If distance is never allowed to lessen, the fight will never go to the ground. This made me think about my first kick-boxing match. I had been matched against an opponent who was nearly equal in experience and weight. Two weeks before the match, I was notified that she had broken some toes and wouldn't fight. I had been training hard and was looking forward to finally test my skill against the unknown. I asked the promoter if he could find me another fighter. He called me back three days before the match and asked if I would fight a lady out of my weight class. Her record was 5-0, and she weighed 155 pounds. At that time, I did not yet understand the importance of weight. In addition, the ring was small (16 X 16 feet), and there seemed to be only a fraction of a second before I found myself squashed up against the ropes, unable to press forward. If I had known then what I know now, I would have trained for position and never allowed her to get near enough to use her weight against me.

We all know that if in the fight game long enough, we will get hit sometime during our martial arts career. Knowing this in advance, which of these two fighters would you rather take a punch from, a heavier fighter or a lighter one?

Most of us would, without hesitation, choose the small fighter over the big one, because he is the least massive of the two. But are you sure that a punch from the smaller fighter would hurt less? There is an interesting twist to this which we will look at later.

Most people would agree that the mountain range separating Colorado and Utah is massive. Some people use mass interchangeably with weight. When we say that something is massive, we generally mean that it is heavy. In physics, the definition of mass is the quantity of matter in an object. If you take a massive object into space, it will become weightless because it is not acted upon by gravity. It will not become "mass-less", however. Mass is also a measure of the inertia of the object. Inertia means resistance to change in motion. The greater the mass, the greater the inertia. This is important to power in the martial arts, because a fighter who possesses a large quantity of mass will become more difficult to stop than a fighter who possesses less mass.

Body Mass In Motion

If you can set a massive object into motion, it will take a lot of force to stop it. One of the principles behind powerful punching and kicking is therefore to keep the mass of your body behind the strikes. If you watch boxing, you will sometimes hear the commentator say that "he is an arm-puncher". This means that the punches will not do much damage, because they are thrown without the weight of the body behind them. Your body has much more mass than your fist alone, and if the strike can originate in the motion of your body, you will be able to generate a great deal of power. There are several ways to do this: take a step forward, for example, or pivot your foot, hip, and upper body in the direction of the strike. An added benefit of stepping or pivoting is that it increases your reach. You can therefore land a strike that initially appears to be too far from the target. The drawback, of course, is that stepping takes time.

Pivoting your foot, hip and upper body increases your reach and adds the weight of your body to punch
(From the archives of Pro-Action Publishing)

Caution: Be aware of your opponent's timing, so that he doesn't counter your forward step with a strike. Your forward motion would then increase the power of your opponent's punch, and would therefore not work to your benefit.

But what if you want to throw a strike that requires a sideways or slightly circular motion, like the hook or the round house kick? How do you place the mass of your body behind such a blow? For best effect, the mass of your body must be moving in the exact same direction as the strike.

Note how Benny "The Jet" pivots on the ball of his foot, placing the mass of his body behind the elbow strike.
(From the archives of Pro-Action Publishing)

Note: A common mistake that many martial artists make is to allow the foot on the same side as the punching hand to raise slightly off the floor. If you hear your instructor say "dig for power", he means for you to place more weight on that foot. This is not the same as being flat-footed. A flat-footed fighter is not as mobile as one who is up on the balls of his feet. To "dig" simply means to place more weight per square inch on that foot.

The power of a round house kick can be increased by taking a lateral step with your supporting foot. You must also allow your upper body to pivot in the same direction as the kick. If your upper body is rigid, you will not be able to bring your hips through, and the kick will almost follow the vertical path of a front kick.

Note how Benny "The Jet" has turned his supporting foot at a forty-five degree angle to the rear. This will help him bring his hips through for power.
(From the archives of Pro-Action Publishing)

To place your body mass behind a strike that follows a vertical path upward, like the uppercut, you must keep your legs slightly bent prior to throwing the strike. This allows you to spring from your knees, placing the weight of your body behind the blow.

Note how Benny "The Jet" keeps his legs slightly bent when throwing the uppercut, and how he pushes off against the floor with the ball of his rear foot for power.
(From the archives of Pro-Action Publishing)

The last of the four major directions in which a strike can be thrown is downward. When throwing this type of strike, your body weight must drop for power. An added benefit is that the force of gravity will work to your advantage.

Note how "The Jet" drops his weight for power when throwing the downward strike.
(From the archives of Pro-Action Publishing)

Weight is beneficial in fighting because of the momentum it can produce. If you can utilize the weight of your body, your strikes will be more powerful than if you rely on muscle strength alone. Momentum is also increased whenever you add motion in the direction of the strike.

Here, Benny "The Jet" is shown using body momentum by pushing off with his rear foot and moving in with the strike.
(From the archives of Pro-Action Publishing)

Instead of using his arm only, Benny "The Jet" relies on the entire weight of his body. This makes for a more powerful strike, but it also takes more energy than throwing with your arm only, so there is a trade-off. Also, be careful not to jam your own strike by getting too close to your opponent before unleashing it.

To add body momentum, the technique has to start in your lower body. When we get tired, it often feels as if our legs are lagging behind. That's also a reason why leg strength is important to power. The legs are used to advance you forward. If the movement starts in your upper body, you will be unable to bring power to the strike, because the upper body will be working on dragging the lower body with it.

We have now looked at how to keep the mass of your body behind a strike that is thrown forward, sideways, upward, and downward. There are, of course, several variations with angles that fall in between these four major ones, including spinning techniques which rely on both linear and circular motion. This is where we need to employ the concept of vectors and resultants, and the concept of rotational inertia, which we will discuss later.

Working With Momentum

Shortly after I started in kick-boxing, my instructor asked me to hold a kicking shield so that he could demonstrate the stepping side thrust kick to the rest of the class. I grabbed the shield and watched him take a few steps back for distance. The next thing I remember is being sprawled out on my back on the floor, my body still tingling from the power of his kick. "If you were going to run through a closed door," he said, "you wouldn't start running, then come to a stop in front of the door, and then bump your shoulder into it, would you?"

To increase the power in your strikes, you must add motion. But any time you start an object in motion and then attempt to stop it, you must overcome inertia. When you restart the object in motion, you must again overcome inertia. Overcoming inertia takes energy and is destructive to power. So once you have started a strike in motion, you must continue that motion through the target with no stopping in between.

Momentum is defined as the product of the mass of an object and its velocity. Velocity is often used interchangeably with speed. The difference, however, is that velocity also has direction, while speed is simply a measure of how fast something is going. Take a look at the following equation:

Momentum = mass (weight) X velocity (speed). Let's say for simplicity that we give the momentum the number 1000. Let's also say that we give the fighter a weight of 200. What would his speed be? When you plug these numbers into the equation, you will see that you must time the weight by 5 in order to arrive at 1000. We can therefore say that: **1000 = 200 X 5.** If the fighter weighed less, say 125 instead, his speed would have to increase in order to reach the same momentum: **1000 = 125 X 8.** So, a lightweight fighter must move faster in order to achieve the same momentum as a heavyweight.

If you are asked to run a distance of five yards as fast as you can, and then to run a distance of one-hundred yards as fast as you can, you are more likely to reach your highest speed somewhere in the second run, because you have more time and distance in which to accelerate. A higher speed will give you more momentum, which will make you more difficult to stop.

The power of a strike will increase if it has a longer distance during which to build speed. Test this concept by throwing a punch with your arm already half extended. Then throw a punch from your shoulder. The additional distance to your target will give your fist more time to build momentum. This is also why kicks thrown with the rear leg usually seem more powerful than kicks thrown with the lead leg; the distance to the target is longer.

In the pictures below, the cross-over side thrust kick allows Benny "The Jet" to advance on his opponent and increase the power in the kick through his forward momentum. Note how he is dropping his weight slightly by bending at the knees and waist. From this lower position, his knees become like a spring, allowing him to gain explosiveness. Impact should happen slightly before the leg is fully extended. This gives the kick a "deeper" effect by sending the energy through the target, and not merely hitting the surface.

Benny "The Jet" executes a cross-over side thrust kick by lowering his weight and springing from his knees.
(From the archives of Pro-Action Publishing)

Are there any exceptions to this? Of course there are. Take the uppercut, for example. Assuming that the strike is thrown mechanically correct, which uppercut will be more powerful, the lead or the rear? According to the principle above, the rear uppercut should be more powerful. However, when throwing the uppercut, the distance of importance between your fist and the target is not horizontal distance but vertical distance. And because your rear hand is farther away horizontally than your lead hand, you will not be able to place as much body mass behind that punch vertically as you will with your lead uppercut. A rear uppercut thrown vertically straight will miss its target, because it will not be lined up with your opponent's chin. A rear uppercut must therefore be thrown at a diagonal angle upward. The lead uppercut, however, is lined up (or nearly lined up) and allows you to place the full weight of your body behind it. Think about this!

Because of its vertical path, the lead uppercut allows you to keep the full weight of your body behind the strike.

The rear uppercut is farther away from the target and must be thrown at a slight diagonal angle upward.

Lowering your weight adds to your balance (low center of gravity and wide base = stability). When throwing a strike that is angled upward, like the uppercut, dropping your weight also allows you to push off for more explosiveness.

Benny "The Jet" drops his weight and springs from his knees to add power to the uppercut.
(From the archives of Pro-Action Publishing)

Lowering your weight is also a great demonstration of how you can combine defense with offense and create more power through your defensive move. Let's say, for example, that your opponent throws a punch, which you weave under by bending at the knees. Naturally, you have to come back up again. But you now take advantage of your defensive move and throw an uppercut within the upward movement. Your body has to reset into your fighting stance. This is what I refer to as "catching two flies with one swat"; defense creates offense.

The principles of power often seem to contradict. For example, it is better to be heavy than to be light, but it is also better to be fast than to be slow. A heavy fighter has a harder time gaining speed than a lightweight. If you are heavier than your opponent, you should strive toward using that extra weight to your advantage without letting it become a burden.

The pictures below are a demonstration of how you can benefit from your weight rather than from your speed. Benny "The Jet" is relying on the forward momentum of his body (delivering the kick with his shin, with full body weight behind it) instead of the speed and snap of his leg. Note also the jump, which makes it easier for him to advance forward with explosiveness.

Benny "The Jet" delivers a round house kick with the shin.
(From the archives of Pro-Action Publishing)

A heavy fighter usually has the advantage at close range, where the lightweight would have difficulties out-muscling him. A strike that is thrown from too tight a distance, however, will lack extension and power will be stifled. A strike that is thrown from too far out will lack penetrating force. When learning to judge proper distance for your hand techniques, you should pay attention to the length of your arms, and the fact that a strike that is thrown mechanically correct, with the weight of the body behind it, will have better reach than one which is not. Tiny adjustments in distance will be necessary throughout the constantly dynamic fight.

Once you have learned to use your mass and velocity against your opponent, you should now learn to use your opponent's momentum against himself. Which would have more impact: driving a car at 30 miles per hour into a stationary object, or driving a car at 30 miles per hour into another car that is moving toward you, also at 30 miles per hour? Which would have more impact: getting hit by your opponent's straight right, or walking forward and into your opponent's straight right?

Leaping knee kick by Benny Urquidez
(From the archives of Pro-Action Publishing, photo by Stuart Sobel)

In the picture below, Benny "The Jet" slips his opponent's punch, simultaneously moving in with a jab to his opponent's mid-section. This is another example of adding momentum, or what I call "catching two flies with one swat."

"Catching two flies with one swat."
(From the archives of Pro-Action Publishing)

Using the principles of physics, Benny "The Jet" takes advantage of both his own and his opponent's momentum, while accomplishing defense and offense at the same time. He has also timed the strike to connect when his opponent is on one leg, either in the process of stepping or in the process of throwing a kick. Being on one leg means that your base is narrow and your stance is not as stable. This is a very bad time to absorb the power of a strike.

Speeding Up Your Punches

When the instructor paired us up to spar in karate class, he told my opponent: "Watch out for her; she's got mongoose blood in her!" Later, when I started in kick-boxing, my instructor sneered and said that he saw my kicks coming three days ago, and that my punches were so slow it's like "waiting for water to boil".

The speed of your hand techniques depends on many factors. Some people's physical makeup and inherited abilities enable them to throw faster punches than others. But like most things, speeding up your techniques is mostly a learned trait, which you can attain with diligent practice.

Some factors that need to be considered when working on your hand speed are:

- **Economy of motion.** The less wasted motion, the faster the strike. Avoid pulling back prior to throwing the strike, or throwing the strike wide. The "pulley effect" is also part of the economy of motion concept. As one hand starts on its way back, the other hand should start on its way out. This will have the effect of your hands "helping" one another and will decrease the beat between strikes.

- **Overcoming inertia.** It takes energy to start your fist in motion, but it also takes energy to stop it once it is moving. The faster you can throw your initial strike, the faster the rest of the strikes in your combination will be. The first strike tends to set the pace. It takes more energy to increase the speed throughout a combination than to simply maintain a speed that has already been set.

- **Avoid falling into opponent's rhythm.** In regard to power, the primary reason for wanting to increase the speed in your strikes is because a faster strike has more momentum. A secondary reason to be faster than your opponent is because it allows you to overwhelm him and beat him to the opening. It is easy to fall into your opponent's rhythm, however. If he throws his strikes at a certain speed, for you to defend against them, you must block or bob and weave at that same speed. But as soon as you have finished your defense, you must speed up your offense. You will now be working with two different speeds: a slower speed which is in tune with your opponent's speed, and which will enable you to defend against his strikes. And a faster speed for your offense, which will enable you to beat your opponent to the opening.

One thing that often seems to inhibit our hand speed is the inability to relax in the upper back and shoulders. Whenever we get ready to throw a punch, the body has a natural tendency to tense the muscles involved in throwing that punch. This tensing will stifle speed and keep us from sending the power of the punch through the target. In other words, we will hit the target but stop short power wise. The punch will feel more like a push.

Note: Because of the impulse, a push is not as powerful as a punch that is "snappy". Impulse is defined as the change in momentum. We will look at this in greater detail later.

The reversal of motion, as when pulling the hand back in defense or in preparation for a second blow, also becomes more difficult when the muscles in the back and shoulders are tense. Because it takes energy to stop a punch in motion, and because a punch must be stopped completely before it can reverse direction, it becomes especially important to stay relaxed.

A punch that is thrown truly relaxed will be thrown with ease and with the punching arm almost fully extended at impact, and will seem effortless.

Caution: Staying relaxed in your shoulders does not mean to allow your hands to drop. Your guard must stay high for protection. When shadow boxing, pay attention to where your shoulders and back feel strained or tense. Work on keeping your shoulders down and relaxed, yet keeping your guard high.

When your opponent is unable to defend against the punches thrown at him, sensory overload will occur. This usually happens when throwing lengthy combinations that are consistently faster than your opponent's. Blocking all strikes at this level becomes almost impossible, and some of your strikes will land. Staying relaxed will help you throw your combinations in spurts to create this effect.

Another interesting concept is that there is usually one fighter dominating the fight through speed, and the fighter who is slower will subconsciously resign to the fact and be unable to bring his strikes up to par. If this is brought to the slower fighter's attention, either through a trainer or through his own mental determination, and he suddenly increases the speed in his strikes, the fighter who was originally faster will now start getting hit. As a result of getting hit, he will have a tendency to slow his strikes to the pace his opponent was at earlier during the fight (this is more of a mental issue than a physical one). This may well reverse the domination of the fight from the faster fighter to the slower fighter (who has now become the faster fighter). If you are originally faster than your opponent, and your opponent suddenly picks up speed, you must increase your own speed and determination even more to keep him from taking the fight from you.

The Power Of The Sideways Stance

When moving or stepping forward to close distance, we sometimes have a tendency to square our stance. This happens because of the many tiny steps involved in stepping, and often happens unknowingly. When it is time to throw the punches, they will be lacking in power because we are unable to keep the full weight of our body behind the blows. Because the fist is connected to the arm, which is connected to the shoulder, we must strive toward getting as much of our body weight behind the punch as possible. In a square stance, only a very small portion of the body weight will be behind the punch (basically just the weight of the shoulder). In a sideways stance, most of the body weight will be behind the punch.

The fighter on the left does not have the full weight of his body behind the blow, and can therefore not generate as much power as the fighter on the right. Which of the following three fighters will be able to generate the most powerful punch?

The fighter on the left carries his elbows behind his body and can therefore not utilize the full benefit of his body mass. In addition, he is leaving his head open for blows. The fighter in the middle carries his elbows too far from his center of mass and is leaving the sides of his body exposed. The fighter on the right is in a good sideways stance with his guard high for protection and his elbows in front of his body for power.

Mass And Momentum Quiz

1. What is the difference between mass and weight?

Mass is a measure of the amount of matter in an object. Weight is how heavy an object is when acted upon by gravity. You can be weightless, but you cannot be massless.

2. Name three ways in which you can place the weight of your body behind your strikes.

A. Take a step forward with your strike.
B. Pivot your foot, hip, and upper body in the direction of the strike.
C. Fight from a sideways stance instead of a square stance (horse stance).

3. When throwing a hook, why should the elbow of the hooking arm stay in front of the body?

To generate power in your strikes, you should rely on body rotation. The body is heavier than the fist and arm, and the move should therefore originate in the body. If the elbow of the punching arm stays behind the body, the elbow must "catch up", and you can therefore not utilize the full weight of the body for power.

4. When is it easiest to utilize body rotation and why: when your hook is a wild swing (sometimes called the "haymaker" or "John Wayne" punch), or when your elbow stays tight to your body?

Any time anything "sticks out" from the center of your body, you must overcome rotational inertia (more about this later). When executing a technique which employs circular motion (hook, round house kick, spinning back kick, etc.), you should keep all body parts as close to your center as possible. This will enable you to accelerate the spin, so that the strike, when released, will happen at its maximum speed. Speed, in turn, translates into power.

Study a video of boxer Mike Tyson. Mike Tyson has the ability to create extreme power in his hooks, because of the way he throws his whole body into the technique. When throwing the hook, try to keep your arm very tight to your body. Then explode with a short jump to increase the momentum of the technique.

5. Once you have started the motion of a strike, it is important to keep it going. Why?

Any time you change the state of motion (from rest to moving, from moving to rest, or slowing down or speeding up), you must overcome inertia. This takes energy and is destructive to power.

6. What is the difference between speed and velocity?

Speed simply tells how fast something is going. Velocity also has direction. This becomes important to the focus of power. If the power of a strike is allowed to split into two or more directions, maximum power in the intended direction cannot be achieved.

7. If you are less massive than your opponent, can you still obtain the same amount of power?

You can increase power by throwing your strikes at a higher speed. This concept will become especially important when we start learning about kinetic energy in a later chapter.

8. How can you use your opponent's momentum against himself?

Time your strikes so that your opponent steps into them. Or if throwing a knee strike, grab your opponent around the neck and pull him forward and into your strike, as you see in Mauy Thai bouts.

9. Name four ways in which you can speed up your strikes?

A.   Use striking that is economical. Avoid any wasted motion.
B.   Once you have started a combination, it takes less energy to keep it going than to stop and then restart a second combination.
C.   Avoid falling into your opponent's rhythm. Mentally, you must be aware of both your own and your opponent's rhythm and force yourself to stay one beat ahead.
D.   Learn to relax.

Glossary

Impulse-The change in momentum. The faster you can change the momentum, the greater the impulse, and the greater the power.

Inertia--Resistance to change in motion. An object at rest tends to stay at rest; an object in motion tends to stay in motion.

Kinetic Energy-Half the mass times the speed squared. Kinetic energy depends on the mass and the speed of the object. If a fighter can double his speed, he can quadruple his kinetic energy. Kinetic energy has a great capability of doing damage.

Mass-The quantity of matter in an object. When acted upon by gravity, we can use mass interchangeably with weight.

Momentum-The product of the mass of an object and its velocity. The heavier the object, and the faster it travels, the greater the momentum.

Resultant-The sum of all vectors. When throwing a strike, we should strive towards making the resultant as long as possible.

Rotational Inertia-Resistance to change in an object that is rotating. It takes a force to change the state or direction of rotation.

Sensory Overload-By striking and kicking with explosive combinations to as many targets as possible in the shortest amount of time, you will create "sensory overload" and send your opponent into a state of confusion and chaos.

Vector-An arrow symbolizing the strength and direction of a force. The longer the arrow, the stronger the force. For maximum power, all vectors must point in the direction of your strike.

Velocity-A measure of the speed of an object and its direction.

CHAPTER 3
Direction

F = ma, An Unbeatable Combination

The best lightweight fighter in the world will be defeated every time by an unranked heavyweight in a bar brawl. True or false?

When stepping on the gas pedal in a car, you will accelerate. If you were a passenger riding in this car, and you had your eyes closed, you would still know that acceleration was taking place because you would suddenly lurch toward the rear of the car. Acceleration is usually associated with building speed, but in physics it also applies to decrease in speed as well as changes in direction. If somebody pulled out in front of you and you stepped on the brakes to avoid a collision, you would now lurch forward instead. Likewise, when you drive up the clover leaf on-ramp to the highway, you will feel your body slide to the outer part of the curve. As mentioned earlier, speed is a measure of how fast you are going, while velocity is a measure of how fast you are going as well as which direction you are moving in. **Acceleration** is then defined as the rate at which velocity changes.

In martial arts, the faster you can accelerate in the direction of your punch or kick, the more power you will produce. This can be demonstrated through the equation F=ma, where **F** is the force; **m** is the mass; and **a** is the acceleration. We have already talked about how a greater mass (heavier fighter), can produce a more powerful strike by placing the weight of his body behind the strike. We have also talked about the importance of speed, and how a fast strike has more power than slow strike. If you can accelerate a strike so that it builds speed with the moment of impact occurring at the highest speed, the force (power) will be even greater. We can also say that a given force divided by a small mass produces a large acceleration. For simplicity, let's say that your punch has a force of 1000 and a mass of 10. What is the acceleration? We can use the equation F=ma: 1000 = 10 X acceleration, or we can say that the acceleration = 1000/10, which is 100. The same force divided by a large mass produces a smaller acceleration: 1000 = 100 X acceleration, or the acceleration = 1000/100, which is 10. If both the mass and the acceleration are large, the force will be even greater. For example, a mass of 100 and an acceleration of 100 is equal to a force of 10000. We can see now why power seems to increase with weight, and why full contact fighting like boxing and kick-boxing always utilize weight classes.

But will the best lightweight fighter in the world really be defeated every time by an unranked heavyweight in a bar brawl? What is the smaller fighter to do when the fight isn't governed by rules and restrictions in weight?

We have talked about the benefits of mass, and how a massive object has more momentum and is therefore more difficult to stop. But a massive object also has more inertia (resistance to change in motion). It is more difficult to stop the motion of a heavy fighter than that of a lightweight, but it is also more difficult to start or accelerate the motion of a heavy fighter. This is why lightweights are often faster than heavyweights. Just watch boxing and you will see for yourself.

Speed translates into power. The faster the speed, and the faster the acceleration, the more power. So you see, there is again a trade-off. A lightweight fighter can produce the same amount of power as a heavyweight, but his punches and kicks must be faster to make up for the lack of sufficient mass. Later, when we get into kinetic energy, we will see how speed can be even more devastating than weight.

Speed In Combinations

Because of the additional mass, a big and strong fighter can be very methodical in his fighting and throw his strikes at a fairly slow pace. But a smaller fighter must rely on speed to create power. When throwing combinations, you should therefore work on decreasing the beat between punches and on ending the combination with a "power strike", usually a rear strike where you can build momentum through distance. If you get tired and need to rest, then rest between combinations.

The higher the speed of a strike, the more power it will generate. You should therefore try to accelerate your strikes with the moment of impact coming at the highest speed. A combination that involves strikes in different directions is difficult to build speed in, because every time you start or stop or change an object's state of motion, you must overcome inertia. That's why it is more difficult to throw a jab followed by lead hook off that same hand, than to throw a jab followed by a rear cross. The jab and the rear cross both go in the same direction, while the jab and the hook have perpendicular paths.

The only way you can change direction without stopping and restarting again is through circular motion. A combination, however, does not consist of strikes only. If you can think of every move as a part of the combination, then you can also combine blocking, slipping, and bobbing and weaving with your offense. Some of these moves are by nature circular, like the bob and weave. You can now utilize the circular motion of this defensive move to set for offense without stopping the motion.

Let's look at the uppercut which can be thrown in two ways: separated from the move that precedes it, or within the move that precedes it. A bob and weave to the left followed by a left uppercut, for example, must be broken down into two moves: First, bob and weave to the left (the body has now set for the uppercut). Then, reverse direction back towards the right along the same path, and throw the left uppercut. It's like the lower half of a circle, or a "smiley face".

Note: A bob and weave is not the same as a slip and weave. Bobbing is the vertical motion of your body and weaving is the horizontal motion. A bob and weave is therefore a combination of vertical and horizontal motion; hence the "smiley face".

You can also throw the uppercut in one continuous motion and build speed throughout. This is done by initiating the move with a left slip instead of a bob and weave. You have now moved your head off the attack line along which your opponent's strikes are thrown. Without stopping the motion, continue into a bob and weave back to your right, and throw the left uppercut.

Benny "The Jet" slips a jab to the left. He then weaves back to the left and throws the left uppercut within the motion of the bob and weave.
[From the archives of Pro-Action Publishing]

As long as there are no opposing movements and you throw strikes that naturally follow one into another, it will take more energy to stop and then restart a combination than to simply keep going. Try the following exercises when practicing punch combinations:

- Evaluate which strikes that naturally follow others. Usually strikes that feel good, in which you are in a balanced stance, and where there are no opposing movements in body mechanics, will be powerful. Alternating strikes are some of the easiest to throw because your body will automatically "set" for the next strike. For example, throw a straight punch with your lead hand, followed by a straight punch with your rear hand.

A jab followed by a rear cross is a "natural" combination, utilizing alternating strikes.
(From the archives of Pro-Action Publishing)

- Work on the "economy of motion" principle, where one strike helps the other. Think of it as a tram going up a mountain. Both the gondola at the bottom and the one at the top will start their motion simultaneously, and will pass each other at the halfway mark. To duplicate this when punching, throw your lead hand, and as soon as it starts on its way back to the guard position, your rear hand should start on its way out.

- Two strikes that employ different directions are the most difficult to attain a natural flow in, especially if both strikes are thrown with the same hand. An example of this would be a straight lead hand punch followed by a lead hand hook. The first punch follows a straight path forward, while the second punch is thrown at an angle perpendicular to the first. Attaining power in this combination requires a very quick move with your body to "reset" the first straight strike before it can again start in the motion of the hook. This combination also requires more energy because you must completely stop the first strike before your hand can change direction.

The jab/lead hook combination employs two different directions, and is therefore more difficult to find a natural flow in.
[From the archives of Pro-Action Publishing]

The combination that Benny "The Jet" demonstrates on the double end bag is one of the more difficult combinations to throw with "crispness". To be successful, you must be careful not to split the resultant into two or more vectors (more about resultants and vectors later). Each strike has to come to a complete stop before the next strike can be started. The reason for this is that the jab, the lead hook, and the lead uppercut are all thrown with the same hand and in three different directions. When going from the jab to the hook, and from the hook to the uppercut, if the motion is not completely stopped before starting the next strike, you will automatically employ circular motion. The benefit of circular motion is that you can allow your strikes to continuously build speed without having to overcome inertia at every start and stop. The danger of circular motion however, is that unless the strike is thrown absolutely straight at the moment of impact, maximum power cannot be attained.

Benny "The Jet" throws three different lead hand strikes, each time employing a different direction.
[From the archives of Pro-Action Publishing]

To attain power, Benny "The Jet" must ensure that his body weight is directly behind each strike (forward with the jab, to the right with the left hook, and upward with the uppercut). If he fails to reset his body's balance between each strike, the next strike will be thrown using arm power only. If he is too "hurried", the next strike may not impact the target straight, and the resultant force will split.

- Relaxation increases speed, and increased speed means increased power. Grab a set of light handheld weights, five pounds each, for example- and alternate left and right punches in the air as fast as you can do this for three two-minute rounds with one minute rest in between. To get the most benefit from this exercise, be sure to bring your hands all the way back to your shoulders between each punch. Once your arms get a little tired, you are less likely to tense your muscles when punching. Be careful not to hyper-extend the elbow by snapping the strike on its way out.

- Put your gloves on and punch the heavy bag with straight left and right punches for three one-minute rounds with one minute rest in between. Focus on relaxation by striking as fast as you can without stopping. When it begins to hurt, do not give in to your desire to slow down. This exercise is supposed to tire your muscles.

When throwing a punch combination, your speed and power should build continuously. This will allow you to end with a strong punch. Most fighters find it easier to throw a multiple punch combination than a multiple kick combination. This is because our hands are naturally faster and more precise than our feet. Because of this, fighters often throw their kicks "isolated". They throw a kick at the beginning of a punch combination, and then pause briefly before beginning to punch. Or they throw a punch combination, then pause and throw a single kick, then pause again and throw another punch combination. As a result, powerful kicks in combinations are seldom seen. Many fighters don't throw multiple kicks at all, but rely solely on single kicks. The drawback of this is that the movement must be stopped and restarted many times, which takes energy and is likely to tire the fighter. In addition, the kicks will often be telegraphed because they are not blended in with the rest of the technique. Try the following exercises when practicing multiple kicks:

- Have a partner hold a kicking shield. Throw ten round house kicks in rapid succession with your lead leg. Your foot must come to a complete stop between each kick before reversing direction. This exercise takes energy and requires relaxation for speed.

- Practice multiple kicks on the heavy bag. As the bag swings, do not attempt to stop it, but adjust to the angle or distance lost or gained by taking tiny steps around the bag. Throwing multiple kicks effectively requires very good timing, coordination, mechanics, and speed.

Note: There is a difference between throwing a multiple kick combination, or simply throwing many single kicks.

- Start the combination with a punch and evaluate which type of kick that would most naturally follow. Because your legs are longer than your arms, unless your opponent steps back to give you distance, some kicks, like the side thrust or spinning back kick, may feel crowded if thrown after a hand combination.

- The round house kick can be thought of as a "universal kick", which can be thrown with ease at the beginning, middle, or end of almost any punch combination. This is because the round house kick follows a curved path and does not, in the same way as other kicks, rely on distance between you and your opponent. If you are far away from your opponent, you may connect with the instep or ball of your foot. If distance is middle range, then connect with your shin. If distance is very close, you may convert the round house kick into a round house knee strike.

The Resultant Force

Power relies not only on force, but also on direction. To obtain maximum power, we must ensure that the sum of all vectors is as long as possible and in the direction we wish to throw the strike. A vector is the combination of the magnitude (strength) of the force and its direction, and is symbolize by an arrow. ———————▶

When throwing a punch which is focused straight forward, and with all of your body weight behind it for power, the resultant force will be in the direction of the punch. But if you throw a punch while simultaneously taking a step back, the punch will lose much of its power because the resultant will be split with one vector going forward and one back.

Think of it this way: A vector is illustrated by an arrow pointing in the direction of the force, with the length of the arrow representing the strength of the force. When you throw a punch, the vector of power can be thought of as being parallel with your arm and in the direction of the punch.

The vector of power is parallel with the fighter's arm and in the direction of the punch.

To calculate the power, all vectors in any given situation must be added, with the ones going in opposite directions subtracted. The final result of this addition is called the resultant. If the punch is thrown absolutely straight with the full weight of the body behind it, the resultant will be at its maximum. If the fighter takes a step back while simultaneously throwing a punch forward, we will have two vectors in opposite directions. When we add these two vectors (subtract the rearward one from forward one), the result force will be less than in the first example, and the punch will therefore not be as powerful. When two or more vectors are going in different directions, the power can therefore not be attatined. A few examples of this would be:

- Leaning back excessively when throwing a kick. Only lean back enough to keep your balance

- Looping a punch. A jab or rear cross should come straight out from the guard position. A common mistake is to raise the elbow prior to punching. In addition to not allowing you to keep the full weight of your body behind the strike, this will also create a vector towards your centerline. Some power will therefore go straight toward the target, and some toward your centerline. The power vector striking the target will now be shorter that the resultant, and maximum power cannot be attained. Another common mistake is to loop the punch slightly downward when retrieving the fist after impact.

- The spinning back kick is especially interesting because of its combination of circular and linear motion. When initiating the kick, the spin should be used to accelerate it. But when the kick connects, your leg must be absolutely straight (linear toward the target). Throwing a powerful spinning back kick requires target accuracy and feel for exactly when to convert the circular motion into linear.

Caution: Don't confuse the spinning back kick with spinning heel kick, which is designed to strike its target from the side.

Benny "The Jet" initiates the spin in his upper body.
(From the archives of Pro-Action Publishing)

The circular motion is then converted into linear, with the kick thrown straight.
(From the archives of Pro-Action Publishing)

• Stepping side thrust kick. Some martial artists are taught the crossover side thrust, where you initiate the forward motion of the kick by moving your rear foot in front of your lead, that your legs are crossed. Stepping will close distance and create momentum, but crossing your feet may redirect the path of the kick slightly, setting your hips at a different angle so that the power is no longer projected straight through the target. For fastest gap closure, your step should be as "clean" as possible. I recommend taking a "half-step" only, by bringing your rear foot forward half the distance to your lead foot. This will decrease the risk of telegraphing the kick, or of narrowing your base too much (loss of balance), and splitting the power into two or more vectors.

• The front kick, when thrown vertically straight, will often allow your foot to slide against your opponent instead of kicking "into" him. A good way to practice penetrating force with the front kick is on a heavy bag that is held steady by a partner. Keeping the bag vertically straight will force you to throw the front kick at a slight diagonal angle upward and into your target. There is an exception to this: if your opponent is bending forward, you may throw a front kick that is vertically straight to your opponent's chin. The kick will now miss all of your opponent's body and hit his chin only.

When executing a takedown, it is very important that you focus all energy in the direction you want your opponent to go, or the resultant force will split into two or more vectors and maximum power cannot be attained. If you want your opponent to go down, you must focus all energy toward the ground. Additional power can also be attained by keeping the technique close to your body, and by using your own weight to aid in the takedown.

Gene LeBell drops his opponent to the ground by applying pressure against the wrist and focusing his energy toward the ground.
[From the archives of Pro-Action Publishing]

Note how Gene LeBell keeps the technique very close to his own center of mass, allowing him to use his weight to aid in the takedown. Note also how his focus is toward the ground only. You can see this by the slight hunching of his upper body as he executes the takedown.

The Overhand Projectile

A strike that seems to end many full-contact matches is the overhand strike. The advantage of this strike is that it can be thrown from a tight distance from where you would normally throw a hook or an uppercut. Because of this, the strike is seldom expected, and as your opponent covers in preparation for a hook or uppercut, the overhand strike will find an open target not from the side or bottom, but from over the top. Because of the downward path of the strike, it also allows you to drop your weight and use gravity to your advantage.

$$\text{Force} = \text{Mass} \times \text{acceleration}$$
$$\text{or}$$
$$\text{Force} = ma$$

As demonstrated by Keith Livingston, the overhand strike comes over the top, allowing you to use the force of gravity to accelerate the strike on its downward path.

Caution: The overhand strike employs circular motion, and we must therefore be careful with the resultant force. When the strike connects with the target, the power must come absolutely straight. A common mistake is to pull your fist in toward your body and split the power into two or more vectors.

The overhand strike can be thought of as a projectile, following a curved path. Because of gravity, the overhand strike will accelerate on its downward path. More acceleration means more power. The target should therefore be struck after the overhand strike has reached its maximum height. The curved path of the overhand strike has two advantages:

- It allows you to use the force of gravity, where the vertical vector component becomes longer than the horizontal one on the downward motion of the strike.

- The overhand strike can be thrown from a tight distance where a straight right would not be possible.

A projectile accelerates only in the vertical direction, while moving at a constant horizontal velocity. In the case illustrated below, the vertical component is longest at the beginning and end of the path, with a reduction to zero at the maximum height. The horizontal component is the same everywhere. The actual velocity, and therefore the power, is represented by the resultant, the diagonal vector.

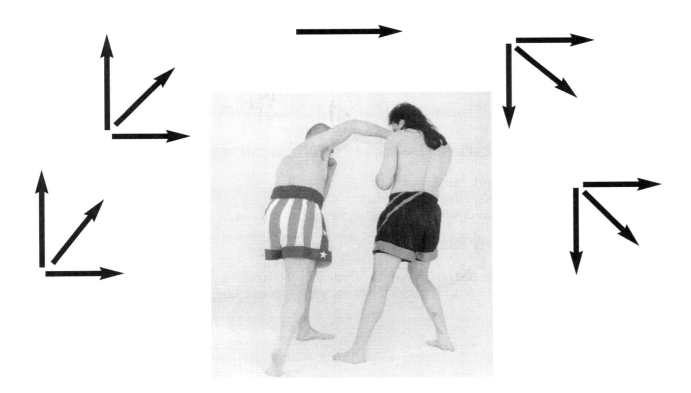

For maximum power, the overhand strike should land when the resultant is at its longest. The strike should therefore land on its downward motion where it can use the force of gravity to its advantage. Gravity by itself may not add significant power to the strike at that short a distance. Power can be further increased, however, by dropping your weight simultaneous with the punch. In addition, when a fighter gets tired, the benefits (or disadvantages) of the force of gravity can be felt more readily.

Inertia And Vector Quiz

1. *Acceleration does not only refer to speeding up. Explain.*

Acceleration is defined as the rate at which velocity changes. But since velocity is defined as the speed and the direction, acceleration is taking place whenever you are speeding up, slowing down, or changing direction (as in circular motion). As martial artists, we are especially concerned with the direction of our strikes. Any "veering off" will split the resultant force into separate vectors.

2. *What is meant by a "natural combination"?*

A natural combination is easy to throw with no awkward movements between strikes. A natural combination has the ability to build speed fast, because there is no stopping and restarting of motion between strikes. In general, natural combinations rely on alternating strikes in the same direction. For example, a jab followed by a rear cross, or a jab followed by a rear leg front kick.

3. *Why is it more beneficial to throw one lengthy combination than to throw many single strikes?*

Throwing many single strikes requires a constant starting and stopping and restarting of motion (overcoming inertia). Throwing a lengthy combination allows you to build speed (which is important to power), with the highest speed occuring at the end of the combination.

4. *Explain why distance is less critical when throwing the round house kick than when throwing a front kick or side thrust kick.*

Because the front kick and side thrust kick are "straight kicks", they rely on the footage between yourself and your opponent. If you are too far away, the kick will not land. If you are too close, you will jam your own kick and stifle power. The round house kick, on the other hand, employs slightly circular motion and is intended to strike your opponent from the side. In addition, impact can be made with your instep, shin, or knee, depending on how far away you are.

5. *Name three mistakes in body mechanics, which have the effect of splitting the resultant into separate vectors.*

  A. Leaning back excessively when throwing a kick.
  B. Looping a punch instead of throwing it straight.
  C. Turning your hips too much when throwing the stepping side thrust kick.

6. *How do you increase the power of the overhand strike?*

The overhand strike follows the path of a projectile, where only the vertical power vector will change in size. The strike should therefore land on its downward motion, where you can drop your weight and use gravity to your advantage.

Glossary

Acceleration–Changes in speed and/or direction. An object that is in motion and changes its direction (a car driving up the clover leaf on-ramp to the highway), will accelerate even if there is no change in speed. You can feel that acceleration is taking place by the way your body lurches forward, back, or sideways.

F=ma–Force equals the mass times the acceleration. A lot of weight and a lot of speed will produce a lot of power. A lightweight fighter can make up for the lack of sufficient mass by being faster than a heavyweight.

Force–Any influence that can cause an object to be accelerated.

Inertia–Resistance to change in motion. An object at rest tends to stay at rest; an object in motion tends to stay in motion.

Kinetic Energy–Half the mass times the speed squared. Kinetic energy depends on the mass and the speed of the object. If a fighter can double his speed, he can quadruple his kinetic energy. Kinetic energy has a great capability of doing damage.

Mass–The quantity of matter in an object. When acted upon by gravity, we can use mass interchangeably with weight.

Momentum–The product of the mass of an object and its velocity. The heavier the object, and the faster it travels, the greater the momentum.

Projectile–An object following a curved path from over the top (overhand strike). In the path of a projectile, only the vertical vector component will increase or decrease in size, while the horizontal vector component remains constant. Because of gravity, the resultant will be at its longest in the downward motion of the projectile.

Resultant–The final sum of all vectors. When throwing a strike, we should strive towards making the resultant as long as possible.

Vector–An arrow symbolizing the strength and direction of a force. The longer the arrow, the stronger the force. For maximum power, all vectors must point in the direction of your strike.

Velocity–A measure of the speed of an object and its direction.

CHAPTER 4
Rotational Speed And Friction
Circular Movement = Power

Jump kicks are often used by martial artists in competition to impress the judges and the audience. Others claim that these kicks have no value except for aesthetic reasons, or to show off. These kind of kicks are often referred to as "flashy". Some claim that jump kicks were originally designed for kicking men off their horses. But today when we don't fight against horseback riders, these kicks are of little value other than to show off our athletic ability. True or false?

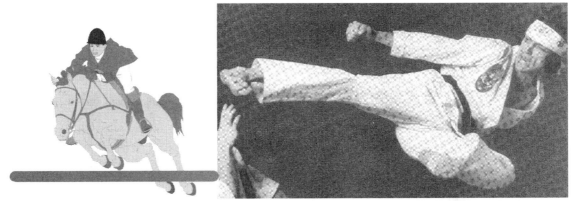

Joseph Jennings executing a flying kick as defense against second opponent on horseback.
(From the archives of Pro-Action Publishing)

An object in motion tends to stay in motion unless acted upon by some outside force. I'm sure that we have all heard of Newton's principles of motion some time during our years in school. But if an object in motion tends to stay in motion, why is it then that if you roll a ball over a flat surface, it will eventually come to a rest? Why doesn't the ball continue in motion forever and ever? Well, it would, unless acted upon by some outside force. The outside force in this case is friction. Friction occurs when two surfaces slide over one another. Less friction means more ease of movement. This becomes important in the martial arts, because different substances have different amount of friction, and if we can reduce the friction as much as possible, our techniques will become faster and thrown with less effort, and will therefore be more powerful.

In curling, friction can be reduced by getting rid of uneven particles on the ice's surface.

Friction is not restricted to solid surfaces, but occurs also in liquids and gases. Friction depends on the nature of the liquid or gas. For example, it is greater in water than in air. Friction in water and air is also less than friction between solid surfaces that slide against one another. But if this is true, then why is there less friction on ice than on pavement? Both are solids, right?

Why can a skater on ice move faster than a person wearing regular shoes?

An ice skater can move faster on ice than a person wearing regular shoes, because the blade of the ice skate is very thin, focusing more weight over a smaller surface area. The pressure of this extra weight lowers the melting point of the ice and changes the state from a solid to a liquid. A liquid has less friction than a solid, and ice will appear more "slippery" because of the thin layer of water between the blade on the skates and the ice. Bet you didn't know that!

But martial artists seldom fight on ice, and even if they did, the slippery low friction surface of the ice hardly seems like an advantage. Having solid ground beneath your feet will give you more friction and better traction, and therefore a decreased risk of losing your balance. As we develop our kicking techniques however, we should become concerned with the friction between our bodies and the air through which they move. Friction in air is less than on a solid surface or in water.

Jump Kicks

When I was teaching karate, we often did "kicks across the room", where I let the students put together kick combinations that the rest of us had to follow. The youngest student in my class, a little boy about eight years old, always wanted to do the tornado kick, which includes both a jump and a spin. This was to the great dismay of the older martial artists who didn't have the same athletic ability. In competition kick-boxing, however, you will mostly see the three basic kicks; the front kick, the round house kick, and the side thrust kick, with an occasional spinning back kick or spinning heel kick. In a full contact environment, jump kicks are time consuming and dangerous to throw. But when analyzed according to the principles of physics, it is found that aside from getting better height out of the jump kick, a fighter can more easily turn his body in the air. This is because there is less friction between the air and the fighter than between a solid surface and the fighter. Easier turn of the body translates into more speed and therefore more power.

For a jump kick to be powerful, impact should come at the "apex", when the jumping foot is at its highest. If the jumping foot is allowed to replant on the floor before the kicking foot makes contact, the power will split into two directions: horizontally into the target, and vertically down into the floor. Power can also be increased by launching your body toward the target. A common mistake is to lean back as the jump is executed, which would have a contradictory effect by splitting the power into two vectors.

When I fought in a kick-boxing match in Canada a few years ago, I felt that I was dominating the fight through every round. When I got back to my corner after the final bell, I was certain that I had won. When they announced a split decision in favor of my opponent, I was utterly confused. Later, her trainer came into my dressing room and said that they had ruled in her favor because she had thrown more high kicks than I had. But this was a leg kick fight! I accepted my loss, but started thinking about how you can increase the power of the low kick even more. A flying high kick, if performed by a person with athletic ability, can have devastating power. But what about a flying low kick? Or is there even such a thing?

In full contact kick-boxing, I often rely on the low kick, because it is fast, easy to throw, and takes little energy. I decided that if the jump could be used as a fake, you would increase your chances of landing the low kick even more. Because the jump kick is generally going to be a high kick, once your opponent sees the need to defend against the high kick, he is likely to "freeze" his upper body in preparation for the blow. To fake a jump high kick, you should look at the high target and initiate the jump. When your opponent tenses, you should now throw the kick low to his legs. Because there is less friction when your body is allowed to turn in the air, the jump will add power regardless of whether the kick is thrown high or low. This adds to the effectiveness of the low kick, yet eliminates the danger of performing the high kick.

Jump, Slide, and Step

The best time to throw a punch or kick is when your opponent is in the process of throwing a kick and is on one leg. There are two reasons for this: First, a fighter is unable to move out of the way when on one leg. Second, balance is greatly diminished when the foundation is narrowed (concept: narrow base = unstable).

Benny "The Jet" lands a perfectly timed jump spinning back kick to opponent Howard Jackson who is on one foot and moving into his opponent.
[From the archives of Pro-Action Publishing, photo by Stuart Sobel]

Another good time to throw a kick is when your opponent is moving toward you. You can now use the principle of adding momentum. Momentum = mass X velocity. In earth's gravity, mass is interchangeable with weight. Velocity is the same as speed, with the added benefit of direction. The impact is greater if struck when stepping toward your opponent than if struck when standing still, because the momentums of both fighters can be added. By timing your strikes right, you can exploit your opponent's strength: his weight and his speed.

The spinning back kick and side thrust kick are two of the most powerful kicks. However, the power of these kicks often fails to mark an opponent for two reasons:

- These kicks require more movement than the front kick or round house kick, allowing the opponent time to move out of range.

- When throwing these kicks, we often have a tendency to move our upper body to the rear, thus splitting the power with some going forward and some backward. Moving your upper body to the rear will also decrease your reach, giving you less penetrating force.

Power can be further increased by training your body to stay "compact". As your body starts to rotate for the spinning back kick, you should simultaneously lower your center of gravity and stay low until impact is complete. Another benefit of staying compact is that it will expose fewer targets to your opponent's retaliation.

When throwing the jump spinning back kick, the same principle applies. If you raise your body, you will have a tendency to lean away from the direction of the kick and split the power into two vectors. When kicking a person who is heavier than you, it becomes difficult to penetrate the target. Staying compact enables you to focus all your energy forward and into the target, using momentum and explosiveness to your advantage.

Because there is less friction between a fighter's body and the air than between his feet and the ground, he can rotate his body for the spinning back kick more easily in the air. Since power in the spinning back kick to a great extent relies on how fast the practitioner can spin, less friction means easier and faster spin. This extra speed does not only add power to the kick, it also makes it more difficult for your opponent to see the kick coming. Even if your opponent sees it, he must first stop his forward momentum, which takes energy, and then reverse direction or side-step to get away from the attack. Varying the shape of the body also allows the practitioner to speed up or slow down the kick. A body that is contracted (made small with no limbs sticking out until it is necessary) can spin faster than a body that is "spread out".

Benny "The Jet" contracts his body before extending the kick against Japanese champion Shinobu Onuki. This allows him to spin faster (less rotational inertia) and attain more power.
(From the archives of Pro-Action Publishing)

Notice also how the kick itself is executed at the apex (the highest point in the jump). This too is done for the benefit of power. If a kick that is designed to go horizontally through the target (like the jump spinning back kick) connects on a fighter's upward or downward motion, the resultant force will split into two or more vectors. In other words, you will have a conflict with the direction of energy, with some energy going into the target, but other (wasted energy) going either up or down, depending on whether you throw the kick while gaining height or while coming back down to the ground.

Benny "The Jet" executes a jump spinning back kick at the apex of the jump.
(From the archives of Pro-Action Publishing)

A jump round house kick also has the potential to be more powerful than a regular round house kick, because it allows the practitioner to rotate his body more freely in the air. The trade off is, of course, that jump kicks require more coordination and athletic ability.

Friction always acts in a direction opposing motion. If you are going forward, friction is going backward, and vice versa. The friction of sliding is somewhat less than the friction that builds up before sliding takes place. That is why it is important not to lock the tires when braking a car. When tires lock, they slide, providing less friction than if they are made to roll to a stop. This concept can be applied to the stepping side thrust kick and the sliding side thrust kick. As your kick makes contact, your supporting foot should slide a few inches forward. This will provide additional power, reach, and momentum.

To preserve maximum penetration, it is important that distance is not increased by leaning back when kicking. Again, your body should stay compact with your center of gravity low. The stepping side thrust kick should be thrown with a small step only to better conceal movement and make the kick more explosive.

Circular Motion

Let's look at Newton's First Law Of Motion: An object in motion tends to stay in motion unless acted upon by some outside force. We have already talked about that the tendency of things to resist change in motion which is called inertia. The law of inertia is extremely important to us as martial artists and applies to a wide variety of techniques. For example, a heavy fighter will be able to generate more power than a lightweight, because the heavier fighter possesses more mass. But mass also relates to inertia. The greater the mass, the greater the inertia. The heavier the fighter, the more difficult it will be to stop his forward motion. But the more difficult it will also be to start any motion at all. And without motion, nothing will happen. The higher the speed, the more power. But if mass helps you increase power, mass also resists the building of speed. One may ask whether it really is to your benefit to be massive in the martial arts.

It is important to understand that it takes more energy to change motion, than to simply continue motion that has already been started. It takes more energy to start and then stop and then restart motion, than to simply keep going. Changing the direction of motion also takes energy, because we now need to apply some force in order to change direction. This becomes important when throwing a lead hook off of a jab, for example. As mentioned earlier, the jab is thrown straight, and the hook is thrown at an angle perpendicular to the jab. That is why this combination seems more awkward than a jab followed by a rear cross.

Take a look at the following concept:

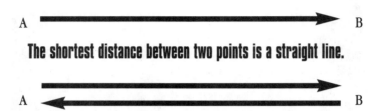

The shortest distance between two points is a straight line.

If you were to walk from point A to point B and back again, you would start at A, stop at B, then turn around and walk back toward A where you would stop. Or you would start at A, stop at B, and then walk backwards back to A.

In the case illustrated above, you must start, stop, and restart motion in order to get from A to B and back to A. This starting and stopping is not only time consuming; you must also overcome the inertia of motion, which wants you to keep going forward without stopping. Take the following common and easy to throw combination: a left jab followed by a right cross. First your left jab comes forward, but in order to pull back and start the right cross on its path out, the jabbing hand must first come to a complete stop, and then the motion of the jab must be restarted in the rearward direction. Because we are trying to build speed for power, this stopping and starting is time and energy consuming. In order to increase the speed and power in our combinations, we need to find a way in which we can change direction easily without having to stop and then restart the motion.

The secret to building speed is in a circle that never stops. Whenever you are moving circular, you can change direction constantly without ever having to stop your motion. Because of this, we are now going to modify the jab/rear cross combination slightly in order to eliminate the stop/start movement.

A

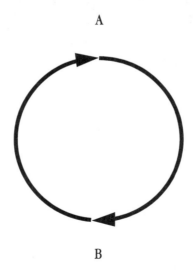

B

This circle enables you to get from A to B and back to A without having to stop motion. The problem, however, is that the shortest distance between two points is a straight line, so moving circular covers a longer distance than moving in a straight line. How do we fix the problem?

A

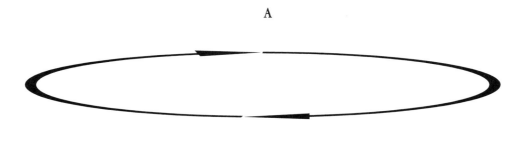

B

This oval enables you to get from A to B and back to A without having to stop motion. The more drawn out the oval is, the less distance you need to cover, and the more economical the strike will be.

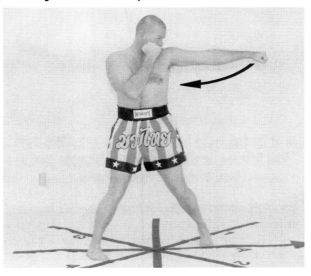

When your jab has landed and it is time to pull that hand back, instead of stopping the motion and then restarting it, try a tiny circle in the downward direction and back toward you. The trick is to make the motion continuous.
(Photo by Martina Sprague)

Caution: Making a tiny circle is not the same as "pawing". Be aware of splitting the resultant into separate vectors. When the strike connects, it must come absolutely straight. If the strike is circular on impact, the power will split with some going into the target and some down toward the ground. After the strike has done its damage however, a tiny circle on its return path will aid in speed when retrieving the punch. The path should not be so circular that your hands drop below the level of the chin, but more of a long, elongated oval. The circle must possess hairline precision, so that you don't split the resultant prior to impact, or expose targets to your opponent's counter strikes.

Rotation Of The Fist

Power and accuracy of a punch can also be increased by rotating your fist to the horizontal position just prior to impact. Your hand now becomes like a drill, pushing through your opponent's guard, and enabling you to take small and well-guarded targets. Because the point in the middle of a rotating system doesn't move, the power is focused over a very small area. This applies to both pointed and blunt objects (your fist). You can test this by attempting to push your fist straight down into a pile of sand. A very large force would be needed to move the sand grains to the sides. But if you rely on a drilling motion, the center of your fist will begin to penetrate.

Rotation of the fist to the horizontal position, as demonstrated by Paul Starling, is a common way to increase power.
(From the archives of Pro-Action Publishing)

When throwing a strike, the rotation should start in your foot, hip, and shoulder. It now seems natural to continue this rotation through your arm and fist. A word of caution: If you start the rotation of your fist too soon, you will have a tendency to raise your elbow prior to punching. This will cause you to throw the strike wide without the mass of your body directly behind it, and with power loss as a result. In addition, a strike that is thrown wide is not as deceptive as one that is thrown "tight".

Because it is not possible to turn the hand a complete 360 degrees, the drilling effect will work best if impact comes slightly before full extension of the arm. Rotating your fist upon impact can also have an abrasive effect, causing cuts on your opponent's face and body. That is the why in boxing and kick boxing the competitors have a light film of vaseline on their face and front upper torso.

Note: Bruce Lee's one-inch punch is thrown with the fist in the vertical position, because the distance to the target is so short (one inch), and twisting the fist to the horizontal position requires slightly more time. The vertical punch gets much of its power from the extension of the elbow and the short explosive move of the body (see page 82).

Torque

Let's say that you are driving your car alone on a desolate road at night, when you get a flat tire. Because you are a person of small build and not very strong, you worry about getting attacked when changing the tire. The tire change must therefore happen quickly. You chock the wheels, jack the car up, and get your wrench from the trunk. But the lug nuts won't budge. You remember when you had the tires rotated last month, and how the repair shop used power tools to tighten the lug nuts. You give it everything you have, but you just don't seem to have the strength. You look around. There is no one near, you don't have a cell phone, and there are miles to the nearest building. You have to get this tire changed. What should you do?

Even though you are a trained martial artist, you never get complacent. You know that awareness is the best defense. You look around and find a three foot long pipe in the ditch. "This can be used as a weapon," you think. Then get a better idea, remembering what your instructor taught you about torque. You grab the pipe, slip it over the wrench handle, and pull. The lug nuts turn. The rest of the tire change is easy, and it's only a matter of minutes before you are moving again safe now, with the pipe stowed in your trunk for future use.

Torque = lever arm X force. This can also be thought of as the product of the distance from the pivotal point and the force that tends to produce rotation.

Torque in the martial arts, is often misunderstood and thought of as an "impact concept". When I was new in the martial arts, my instructor told me that "torque" my hand on impact (meaning to turn the hand form the vertical to the horizontal position) would produce a higher force (see "Rotation Of The First" previous page). But torque does not relate to inpact in the same way as impulse or momentum. Torque is a "leveage concept", and the idea is not to use more force to increase the torque, but to use a longer lever arm, enabling you to use less force to do more damage, at the same time conserving energy. Speed is not even relevent. As a matter of fact, torque can be increased by inching extremely s-l-o-w-l-y. It's how much leverage you have that matters, and not what your force is on impact.

Torque can be thought of as leverage in the pivotal rotational plane. In the picture below, Gene LeBell uses torque against his opponent's elbow joint. The pivotal point is the elbow, the lever arm is the distance from the elbow to the wrist (where Gene LeBell's hand is), and the force is the pressure that Gene LeBell exerts by pulling up on the wrist. The more you increase the distance (the lever arm), the more you increase the torque. This allows you to use a lesser force to produce the same amount of torque. If Gene LeBell was grabbing his opponent closer to the elbow instead of at the wrist, it would be much more difficult to do damage.

Gene LeBell uses torque to control his opponent.
(From the archives of Pro-Action Publishing)

Why is the pivotal point at the elbow and not at the shoulder? Naturally, the pivotal point would be at the shoulder, where the arm is attached to the body. But because the elbow is less flexible than the shoulder, Gene LeBell knows that it will be easier to control his opponent by the elbow. He does this by isolating the elbow (keeping it from moving) with his own elbow. For best results, the force should be applied at a 90 degree angle (perpendicular) to the lever arm. As you can see, the angle between Gene LeBell's arm and his opponent's arm is slightly more than 90 degrees. The torque can be increased by decreasing the angle, or by extending the lever arm.

Torque is also great in throws. The picture sequence below shows Martina Spraque (the author) catching her much bigger opponent's round house kick in the crook of the her arm. Note the 90 degree angle between Martina's arm and her opponent's leg (the lever arm). Martina now extends her arm, at a 90 degree angle to her opponent's leg, and takes him down backwards.

Martina Sprague (the author) catches Keith Livingston's round house kick in the crook of her arm, utilizing torque to throw him off balance.
(Photos by Tom Sprague)

To utilize torque to its fullest, you must catch the kick as far from the pivotal point as possible. The pivotal point is were the leg is attached to the body. It is therefore better to catch the kick close t your opponent's foot rather than close to his hip. Remember, the longer the lever arm (the distance from the pivotal point to the force), the less force you will need to apply for a given amount of torque. If the kick had been caught at the knee joint instead of at the ankle, more force would be needed for this particular type of takedown.

Think about this: If you were to sweep your opponent, would you sweep close to the foot, at the calf, or at the thigh? You would sweep as low as possible, close to the foot, because that would make the lever arm (the distance between the applied force and the pivotal point: your opponent's leg in this case) as long as possible, thereby allowing you to use less force.

The Catch-22

Mass can be described as the quantity of matter in an object. More mass = more powerful strikes. But mass is also a measurement of the inertia or "sluggishness" in starting, stopping, or changing the object's state of motion. More mass = more difficult to set in motion.

Newton's Second Law Of Motion states that the acceleration of an object is directly proportional to the net force acting on the object, is in the direction of the net force, and is inversely proportional to the mass of the object. In simple terms, this says that whereas force tends to accelerate things, mass tends to resist acceleration. So, a heavy fighter must use more force to set himself in motion.

Newton's Third Law Of Motion states that whenever one object exerts a force on a second object, the second object exerts an equal and opposite force on the first. If you hit somebody, technically you will get hit back by his block with an equal amount of force. But if you will get struck back as hard as you strike your opponent, then what's the benefit of striking at all? And why is it that the person executing the strike seldom gets injured, while the person absorbing the strike does? The answer lies in your choice of target and in the physical build of the "striking weapon":

- First, your strike must hit a target that is likely to cause injury.

- Second, you must ensure that your striking weapon is structurally stronger than your target. That's why it is important to curl your toes back when throwing the front kick, to double up your fists tightly when throwing a strike, and to block a leg kick with the muscle slightly to the outside of your shin and not with the bone.

To give your strikes penetrating force, the energy must be focused over a small surface area. Using your hand to block a kick rather than your elbow, for example, has two disadvantages:

- There will be less penetrating force, because of the bigger area of your hand.

- You will leave yourself open, because you must drop the hand from the high guard position in order to use it for blocking a kick.

To sum it up then, we can say that when striking and blocking, you should use parts of your body that are tolerant to impact, and strike parts of your opponent's body that are not.

Rotational Inertia

It has been said that "movement in fighting is circular". If two fighters meet and attack each other head on, the stronger fighter will win. This is because the stronger fighter will have the ability to back his opponent up and to dominate the space in which they are fighting. The intelligent fighter relies on circular movement both when fighting offensively and defensively. When you are the aggressor, using angled attacks instead of straight attacks will give you more open targets, and will confuse your opponent and make it more difficult for him to defend against the attack. When you are the underdog and need to be on the defensive against an aggressive opponent, circular movement will make it more difficult for your opponent to land a good strike.

When fighting in a confined area, whether it is a ring in a tournament, or a room in your house, or another confined area outside, one thing to keep in mind is that the person who dominates the center will dominate the fight. This goes back to the concept of rotational speed in physics. If you study traditional weapons, you probably have a bo staff at home. This simple staff has the advantage of a six foot reach. When performing your forms, you have probably learned how to rotate the bo staff above your head, either by holding on to one end of the staff, or by holding it in the center. The pivot point (where your hand is) will rotate very slowly in relation to the tips, yet the rotational speed stays the same throughout the rotating system. The farther out you are

59

from the center however, the faster your linear speed will be. This bit of knowledge can work both to your advantage or disadvantage. If you can dominate the center of the ring for example, you will conserve much energy compared to the fighter who has to move around you in big circles.

Morihei Ueshiba (master and founder of Aikido) was able to astound multiple attackers by setting them flying, while he himself seemed undisturbed by their attack.

The eye of the storm is where the calm is. The farther you are from the center, the more violent it will be.

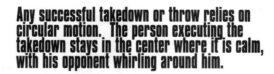

Any successful takedown or throw relies on circular motion. The person executing the takedown stays in the center where it is calm, with his opponent whirling around him.

Because power relies on speed, when working spinning techniques, you will want to strike your opponent with as much speed as possible. When striking with the bo staff, you will want to strike your target as close to the tip of the staff as possible. The tip is farther from the center of the circle, and therefore travels at a faster linear speed. The same concept applies to weaponless spinning techniques (spinning back fist, spinning back kick, spinning heel kick, etc.). When throwing these techniques, you should strike your opponent as close to the tip of the striking weapon as possible, because that's where the highest speed is and therefore the most power. Throwing a spinning back fist for example, and being too close to your opponent, may result in striking him with your elbow instead of your fist. Aside from the fact that the elbow is a vicious striking weapon, it will not be able to generate the same speed as the fist, which is about twice as far from the axis of rotation when your arm is straight. That is why it is also important to extend your arm to the straight position upon impact.

Building speed throughout the spin goes back to the concept of rotational inertia. Again, inertia means resistance to change. Rotational inertia means resistance to change in an object that is rotating (spinning back fist/kick, for example). How then do we overcome the rotational inertia when throwing a spinning technique?

Rotational inertia depends on the distribution of mass with respect to the axis of rotation. This can be demonstrated with a hammer. If you want to balance the hammer on your finger tip, which will be easiest, to balance the hammer on its head or on the shaft? Try it!

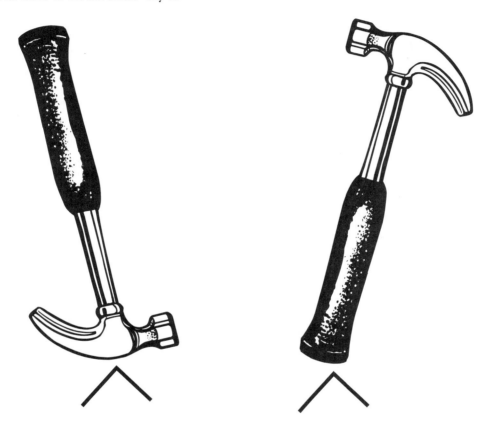

On the shaft is easier because the head-end is heavier. Most of the mass is therefore farther away from the center of rotation (your finger). The greater the distance between the bulk of an object's mass and its axis of rotation, the greater the rotational inertia. This is also why it is easier to balance on a beam or tightrope when you carry a pole. The longer the pole, the easier it is to balance, because the pole has much of its mass away from its rotational axis (center).

So, in what way does this apply to spinning techniques? Well, if a spinning technique has a great deal of rotational inertia, it becomes difficult to set it in motion or to accelerate it. A technique that can't accelerate will lack power (more acceleration = more speed = more power). We as martial artists must therefore find a way to overcome the rotational inertia when initiating a spinning technique. This can be done by keeping the bulk of your mass as close to your center as possible. Keeping your arms and legs tight to your body allows you to spin faster, and when it is time to release the technique it will have more power through this faster speed. Any time anything is sticking out from your body, it will resist the rotation of your body. When initiating the spinning back fist then, you must keep your arms tight to your body, and not extend your arm until it is almost time to land the strike. When resetting after the technique is complete, you should again contract your arm to the tight position. This will aid you in the spin back to your fighting stance. In addition to speeding up the technique, keeping your arms tight throughout the spin will also protect you against your opponent's strikes, in that you will not leave your head and rib area exposed to blows.

Benny "The Jet" starts the rotation of his upper body. Note how his arms stay tight throughout the spin.
(From the archives of Pro-Action Publishing)

Not until it is time to release the strike, does Benny extend his arm.
(From the archives of Pro-Action Publishing)

Whereas rotational inertia aids in balance, it also counteracts speed. The potential loss of balance when throwing the spinning back fist, however, is not large enough to offset the benefits of the extra speed. In the pictures below, by sequentially extending his arm, Benny "The Jet" can increase the power in his strike by using a higher rotational speed (conservation of angular momentum and less inertia). By extending his arm the moment before impact, he will connect with his fist, where the highest linear speed is. High speed = high power.

Benny "The Jet" connects with his fist (the tip of the rotating system) against Japanese champion Genshu Igari where the highest linear speed is.
(From the archives of Pro-Action Publishing)

It is interesting to note that "The Jet" connects with the side of his fist, while some fighters, including myself, like to connect with the back of the fist. The power advantage of "The Jet's" spinning back fist lies in the direction of the strike. The elbow comes up and points at the target, and the strike is then extended in the direction of the elbow, so there is no conflict with the direction of energy. When connecting with the back of the fist however, the elbow is pointed slightly downward, so there would be a slight conflict with the direction of energy. According to the principles of physics, connecting with the side of the fist rather than the back of the fist should be more powerful, providing that the striking weapon is structurally sound.

Unlike the spinning back fist or spinning heel kick, which are comprised of circular motion only, the spinning back kick is comprised of both circular and linear motion. When initiating this technique, you are utilizing circular motion to build momentum for power. But when landing the technique, your leg will be extended straight toward your target (linear motion). Unlike the spinning back fist or spinning heel kick, which strike their target from the side and in the direction of the spin, the spinning back kick strikes its target straight (like a jab or rear cross). When there is a lot of rotational inertia, it becomes difficult to change direction from circular to linear. By keeping your leg tight to your body throughout the spin, this last minute change in direction right before impact will take less effort.

Benny "The Jet" spins his upper body for the spinning back kick (circular motion), then extends the leg straight to the target (linear motion).
(From the archives of Pro-Action Publishing)

So, in addition to speeding up the spin, keeping your leg tight throughout the spin will also speed up your technique once it becomes time to extend it straight into the target. Whenever a rotating body contracts, its rotational speed increases. This is defined as conservation of angular momentum.

Friction And Rotational Speed Quiz

1. In what way can we as martial artists reduce friction without sacrificing balance?

Different substances have different amount of friction. To the martial artist, friction is advantageous some-times but not always. For example, if engaged in a confrontation, you will be better off fighting from a high fric-tion dry surface than on ice. When throwing a technique however, the less friction there is between the tech-nique and the substance through which it moves, the easier it will be to gain speed. You can decrease friction by allowing your body to turn freely in the air. As long as there are no opposing movements in body mechan-ics, balance does not need to be sacrificed.

2. The shortest distance between two points is a straight line. But how can you utilize the benefits of circular motion without increas-ing distance?

You can't! A circle will always cover a longer distance than a straight line. But is it really distance we are con-cerned with? Keep in mind that fighting is a give/take situation, where sometimes it becomes necessary to give something up in order to gain a bigger advantage. The reason you want to use circular motion is because it enables you to increase your speed by eliminating the start/stop movement. The benefit of a sufficient increase in speed will offset the tiny bit of extra distance you need to cover. When throwing your strikes, an oval which is almost like a straight line but not quite, will enable you to increase your speed significantly without increas-ing distance that much.

3. Newton's Laws Of Motion often seem to contradict our efforts in gaining power. For example, you can't strike somebody without being struck back equally hard by the target you strike. How do you inflict damage on your opponent, yet remain unharmed by Newton's Third Law Of Motion?

When striking an opponent, you must use a part of your body that is structurally stronger than the target you are striking.

4. Why is it easier to do sit-ups when your arms are extended in front of your body than when they are clasped behind your head?

When your arms are extended in front of your body, your center of mass is closer to the rotational axis, thus less rotational inertia.

5. Why do we bend our legs more when running than when walking?

Bending your legs helps your body contract, which in turn reduces the rotational inertia, which in turn allows you to speed up for the run.

6. Why does the dachshund have a faster stride than its owner?

Rotational inertia is dependent on how far the bulk of the mass is located from the axis (center of rotation). Short legs have less rotational inertia than long legs, and can be moved quicker as a result. To demonstrate this grab a set of light hand held weights (3-5 pounds). Hold the weights in your hands with your arms extended straight out to the side. Spin on one foot, then quickly pull your arms in tight to your body. Did the speed of your spin increase automatically? You may even have lost your balance as a result. So, you see, when your body contracts, it becomes easier to gain speed in a spinning technique. This is also important when performing a jump kick that requires a turn of your body in the air (jump spinning back kick, jump round house kick). You can change your rotational speed by making variations in the shape of your body.

Glossary

Acceleration–Changes in speed and/or direction. An object that is in motion and changes its direction (a car driving up the clover leaf on-ramp to the highway), will accelerate even if there is no change in speed. You can feel that acceleration is taking place by the way your body lurches forward, back, or sideways.

Adding Momentum–When two objects move toward each other and collide, the force of impact will be stronger than if only one object is moving, providing that the speed is the same in both cases.

Conservation Of Angular Momentum–Whenever a rotating body contracts, its rotational speed increases. A rotating body will cover the same area within a specified time frame. A rotating body which is "spread out" will cover a larger area than one which is contracted. Therefore, the contracted body will need to spin faster in order to cover the same area.

Friction–Resistance of motion between two solid surfaces, liquids, or gases. Friction is less in air than in water or on ground.

Inertia–Resistance to change in motion. An object at rest tends to stay at rest; an object in motion tends to stay in motion.

Linear Speed–The tip of a rotating system will move faster than the center, even though the rotational speed (revolutions per minute) are the same throughout the system.

Mass–The quantity of matter in an object. When acted upon by gravity, we can use mass interchangeably with weight.

Momentum–The product of the mass of an object and its velocity. The heavier the object, and the faster it travels, the greater the momentum.

Newton's First Law Of Motion–An object in motion tends to stay in motion unless acted upon by some outside force. Martial artists should strive toward throwing a continuous combination, rather than many single strikes.

Newton's Second Law Of Motion–The acceleration of an object is directly proportional to the net force acting on the object, is in the direction of the net force, and is inversely proportional to the mass of the object. Whereas a big force produces a large acceleration, a big mass resists acceleration.

Newton's Third Law Of Motion–To every action there is an equal and opposite reaction. You cannot hit someone or something without being hit back with an equal and opposite force.

Resultant–-The final sum of all vectors. When throwing a strike, we should strive toward making the resultant as long as possible.

Rotational Speed–The number of rotations per unit of time (revolutions per minute). In a spinning technique, the revolutions per minute in the center is the same as the revolutions per minute near the tip. However, the tip will move with a faster linear speed because it is farther from the axis. The rotational speed is the same regardless of how far you are from the center, but the linear speed is proportional to the distance from the axis.

Rotational Inertia–Resistance to change in an object that is rotating. It takes a force to change the state or direction of rotation.

Torque–The product of the lever arm and the force. The longer the lever arm the less force is needed to produce a given amount of torque.

Vector–An arrow symbolizing the strength and direction of a force. The longer the arrow, the stronger the force. For maximum power, all vectors must point in the direction of your strike.

Velocity–A measure of the speed of an object and its direction.

CHAPTER 5
Impulse
Striking Through The Target

Have you ever witnessed a board or brick breaking competition in which the practitioner was asked to break the bottom brick while leaving the others intact? Did he succeed? Did he use some kind of magical trick to do this? Did he cheat? It is in fact possible to strike the top brick and break the one on the bottom. Some people call this "extension of ki", or internal energy. I like to call it "transfer of kinetic energy. This kinetic energy" has a deeper effect than simply striking the surface.

As a martial artist, your instructor has probably told you a number of times to strike "through" the target. Those of us who are less schooled in the martial arts may interpret this as your fist is actually going into your opponent's body and through it, maybe even coming out the other side. In physics however, this striking "through" the target means allowing the power of the strike to extend beyond the physical surface and into the opponent's body.

Focusing a few inches beyond the physical surface allows Master Angi Uezu to extend the power of his strike "through" the target.
(From the archives of Pro-Action Publishing)

The definition of **kinetic energy** is energy in motion. This might have been demonstrated to you in physics class in school, where the teacher had a set of balls hanging on strings from a bar. All the balls are touching one another. The ball on the far end is then moved and released. When it hits the next ball, the ball at the other far end pops out. The balls in the middle, however, do not move. This is a demonstration of how energy can travel through a medium.

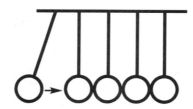 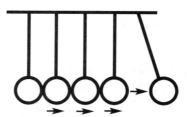

When the ball on the far left is released and strikes the next ball, energy travels through a medium, and the ball on the far right pops out.

In the martial arts, there is a fine line between snapping a punch and pushing it. If a strike is left in contact with the target too long, it will result in a push. But if a strike is snapped back too soon, it will lack proper transfer of kinetic energy; it will merely hit the surface without doing any real damage. To develop full power striking, you must develop a feel for the proper time of impact. Working on relaxation in your strikes will help you with this. A tense strike uses muscular power to reverse the direction of motion upon impact. A relaxed strike on the other hand, takes less energy to throw than a tense strike. Therefore it allows you to "sink" the strike beyond the physical surface and through the target, and to use the target itself to aid in reversing the strike back to the guard position (point of origin).

World champion kick-boxer Benny "The Jet" Urquidez emphasized that "The way you train is the way you react." It is my belief that if you want to develop power for full contact fighting or self-defense, you must train accordingly. Some touch sparring competitions penalize the practitioner for using too much contact. He should only "mark" his strikes with a light to moderate tap. When this is done repeatedly, we train our body to pull the punches, or to judge distance wrongly, or to not extend beyond the physical surface. This holding back interferes with proper energy transfer. As a martial artist, you must therefore evaluate your situation and decide what your goals are. Do you practice for sports? Competition? The street? Kickboxing? Reality fighting? If you do decide that you want to practice for sports/touch sparring tournaments, you can still develop powerful strikes by practicing full power striking on bags or mitts a couple of times a week.

You must now find the fine line in between the snap and the push. That is where the striking weapon is left in contact with the target long enough to allow for proper energy transfer, but not so long that power is diminished.

Decreasing The Time Of Impact In The Grappling Arts

Impulse is defined as the force times the time interval. We have already talked about how the momentum of an object will change if either the mass or velocity (speed) changes. We have also talked about how mass, speed, and momentum all relate to power. Impulse can also be defined as the change in momentum. A large change in momentum in a long time requires a small force. A large change in momentum in a short time requires a large force. To attain power in the martial arts, we should strive toward producing a force that is as large as possible. When throwing a punch that suddenly stops or reverses direction upon impact, the shorter the time in which the momentum is changed (reduced to zero), the larger the force.

Let me ask you this: If you were to jump from a five story building, where would you rather land, on the concrete sidewalk below, or in a net that the fire department had brought out to your rescue? We know that it would hurt less to land in the net, but why is that? The reason for this is that the time during which your momentum changes (during which you come to a stop) is much longer when landing in the net than when hitting the concrete sidewalk. The net has "give", which slows you down little by little. When the time is long, the force is small, and you will therefore walk away uninjured.

Try this exercise: Get up on a chair and jump off, landing on your feet. Why did you bend your knees? Because it increases the time of impact, and your body will gradually absorb the force. If you lock your knees instead, you will get hurt, even when jumping from a very low height.

Many martial arts employ throwing techniques. It is therefore crucial to the practitioner to learn how to fall without getting injured. Aikido and Judo practitioners get thrown to the floor repeatedly, yet keep from getting hurt. These martial artist have learned to spread the impact over as large an area of their body as possible. The forward roll, for example, utilizes the hand, forearm, and shoulder to gradually and sequentially absorb the shock. This spreads the impact over an extended period of time. More time means less force. It is therefore possible to fall from a considerable height, or to be thrown at a considerable speed without getting hurt.

Note how Gene LeBell absorbs the force sequentially by executing the forward roll.
(From the archives of Pro Action Publishing)

In addition to helping you absorb the impact of the fall, a rolling technique also gives you considerable momentum, which can be used to get back on your feet or to gain distance from your opponent.

The second way to absorb the shock of a fall is to absorb the force all at once by spreading it over as large an area of your body as possible.

Note: The principle of spreading out and absorbing the shock over as large an area as possible applies only to situations that involve a solid surface, as would be the case in most fighting situations. If falling into water, however, the opposite is true, and the force will be reduced by allowing your body to penetrate the surface. Consider a belly splash off a fifteen foot high springboard. Would it hurt? If you made yourself smaller instead, allowing your feet or head to penetrate first, you would come through the fall unharmed.

The amount of control you have over the situation will determine which type of fall you should use. In general, it can be said that if the fall is a result of your own initiative, as would be the case when a fighter is escaping a controlling technique by executing a forward roll, the principle of absorbing the shock gradually and sequentially should be used. The force is absorbed over a long period of time and is therefore lessened (concept: impulse = Ft).

If the fall is a result of your opponent's initiative, as would be the case when a fighter is picked up and thrown, he may not have the option of a rolling technique to break the fall. He should then rely on the second principle of falling; that of spreading the impact over as large an area of his body as possible (concept: pounds per square inch).

In the picture on the left, the martial artist is grabbed in a twist lock (joint lock against the wrist). He escapes the technique by initiating the forward roll (tucking his head and shoulder toward the floor). He decreases the impact of the fall by rolling on his arm, shoulder, and back to absorb the shock gradually. His head never touches the floor.
(From the archives of Pro-Action Publishing)

The practitioner of this type of fall must keep all vital areas from touching the ground. When utilizing the backward break fall, your chin must be tucked down toward your chest to keep your head from hitting first. You should also make sure that your arms are extended and not bent, as you would otherwise absorb the force on your elbows. Slapping the mat simultaneously or slightly before landing, and at an angle away from your body, will help you absorb the force over a greater surface area, while at the same time redirecting the force away from your internal organs.

Gene LeBell executes a backward break fall with a slap at a forty-five degree angle away from his body.
(From the archives of Pro Action Publishing)

When utilizing the side break fall, the force should again be absorbed over as large an area as possible. Note in the pictures below, how Gene LeBell lands on the whole side of his leg and body, and how his arm slaps the mat at an angle away from his body.

(From the archives of Pro Action Publishing)

The next logical step is the front break fall from a standing position. When utilizing this technique, we have a natural tendency to want to "catch ourselves on our hands and knees". To absorb the shock of this type of fall, the hands and forearms must slap the mat a fraction of a second before the body lands. If you land on your wrists, elbows, or knees alone, the force will be absorbed over a very small surface area which is also structurally weak. This will produce a higher force per square inch, and the risk of injury will be greater.

Note, in the picture below, how Gene LeBell prepares to absorb the shock along the palms of his hands and forearms. If the fall was executed from a standing position, his knees would not be touching the ground, and the weight of his body would be supported by the toes and forearms alone.

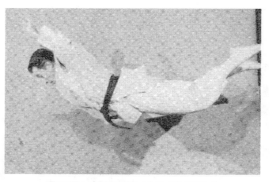

[From the archives of Pro-Action Publishing]

Decreasing The Time Of Impact In The Striking Arts

In a stand-up type fight, going with the motion will increase the time of impact, thus reducing the force. Moving forward into your opponent's punch will hurt more than moving backwards and away. When working on offense, you will therefore want to time your strikes to your opponent's forward movement, making him walk into your strikes. This will change the momentum in a short period of time, thus increasing the force of the blow. For best results, the force should be delivered in as short a time as possible.

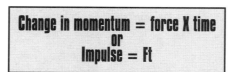

$$\text{Change in momentum} = \text{force} \times \text{time}$$
$$\text{or}$$
$$\text{Impulse} = Ft$$

Impulse = Ft Impulse = Ft

In the picture on the left, Keith Livingston executes a rearward slip to minimize the force in his opponent's blow. In the picture on the right, he makes the mistake of moving forward and into his opponent's strike. Which will hurt more?
(Photos by Martina Sprague)

The force can be increased by striking a target that has very little give. In the picture on the following page, the target is immobilized by pulling on the opponent's arm, while simultaneously kicking to the head. The body is kept from moving back, the time of impact is short, and power is increased. It's not just the power in the kick that works to the practitioner's advantage; it's also the fact that the only "give" that exists is in the opponent's neck, which is an inherently weak area.

Fumio Demura increases the power in his kick by pulling on his opponent's arm.
(From the archives of Pro-Action Publishing, photo by Mary Townsley)

The power in a takedown can be increased by applying pressure against the natural movement of the joints. This will immobilize your opponent, giving the target area very little give. If you execute a strike now, power is increased because of the shorter time of impact against a target that can't move with the force.

Benny "The Jet" uses a shoulder lock to immobilize the target. He then executes a knee strike to the back of his opponent's head.
(From the archives of Pro-Action Publishing)

Since the joints are inherently weak areas in our body structure, a smaller person can use a joint lock to defeat a bigger adversary. By immobilizing the joint and relying on the concept of impulse, he can increase the effectiveness of the technique.

Benny "The Jet" utilizes the ground in conjunction with a shoulder lock to immobilize his opponent. A stomp to the head would now be devastating. When the head has no place to go, the power is absorbed in a very short period of time.
(From the archives of Pro-Action Publishing)

Impulse can also be used to produce power which will help you break free from a lock-up. A chain will break at its weakest link. In the picture below, the opponent's arms around Benny "The Jet's" body can be viewed as a link in a chain. The weakness is where the hands come together. By forcefully spreading his arms, "The Jet" is able to break the grip, free himself, and continue with a counter-attack. For this technique to work, especially for a smaller person, the moves must be executed dynamically. Especially in grappling, where you are in actual physical contact with your opponent, any small move or "intention" can often be felt at its earliest stage. If a person fidgets or applies pressure gradually, it will be easy for the opponent to pick up on this move and increase the intensity of his attack. Breaking free should therefore happen explosively without any prior warning. The shorter the time, the greater the force. If the break free simulates a push, you are not likely to succeed.

Benny "The Jet" escapes a rear bear hug by forcefully spreading his arms.
[From the archives of Pro-Action Publishing]

Reversing Direction By "Bouncing"

Karate practitioners who are into board breaking will be more successful if they can reduce the momentum to zero in the shortest time possible. To break boards or bricks, you should bring your hand or foot swiftly against the board with considerable momentum. Upon impact, the momentum should be brought to zero in a short time. This will produce a large force. An interesting concept is that if your hand or foot is made to "bounce" upon impact, the force is even greater. That is because the impulse required to bring your strike to a stop, and then reverse the motion by "throwing it back again" is greater than the impulse required to just bring it to a stop. When you stop something, the momentum changes to zero; when you reverse its direction, the momentum must again change from zero to a higher number, so the total change in momentum is greater than if you simply brought it to a stop. Remember, impulse = change in momentum. The force is increased because the time of contact is reduced. The impulse is also increased because the direction of the strike is reversed. The impulse, when reversing direction, is supplied by your opponent's body as your hand or foot bounces off it.

The momentum goes from 10 to 0.

"Benny the Jet" initiates a punch with a momentum of ten (for simplicity). When the punch connects, the momentum changes to zero. The total change in momentum is therefore ten. The momentum goes from 0 to 10.

[From the archives of Pro-Action Publishing]

When "Benny the Jet" retrieves his hand back to the guard position, the momentum goes from zero to ten, but in the opposite direction. The total change in momentum when throwing a punch that reverses direction after impact is therefore twenty, or twice that of a punch that stops upon impact and does not reverse direction.

Kenpo Karate practitioners rely on bouncing their strikes off of both their own and their opponent's body. Kenpo Karate is often negatively referred to as a "slap art", where the slaps against your own and your opponent's body are merely looked upon as some kind of fancy show-off. Many kenpo practitioners also claim that these slaps are in reality "checks" against the opponent's blows. But those who understand the underlying principles of physics, will be able to greatly improve the power of their strikes by relying on bouncing to increase the impulse. This can almost be thought of as "adding momentum". When you strike something, it strikes you back, thus producing the bouncing effect. Time of impact is lessened and power is increased.

At a belt promotion in Kenpo Karate, 1991, Martina Sprague (the author) builds great hand speed and power through circular movement and "bouncing" of her strikes off of both her own and her opponent's body.
(Photos by Tom Sprague)

When the Kenpo practitioner allows his own hand to bounce off his own body, he aids in the reversal of motion. He does not have to rely on muscular effort to bring his hand to a stop and then to restart it again in the opposite direction. Instead, he relies on his body to bring the hand to a stop and reverse direction. This will help build speed without using a great deal of muscular effort. The fighter will therefore be faster without getting tired or arm weary. This extra speed in turn, results in an increase in power.

When the Kenpo practitioner relies on the target (his opponent's body) to provide the reversal of motion, the impulse, and therefore the power, is increased. If you subconsciously use your muscles to bring your hand to a stop and reverse its direction, the desired result cannot be attained. The impulse is created through the "bouncing" of your hand against the target. The "snap" has to come from the opposing surface and not from "within". When reversing direction, the impulse must be exerted on the object by something external to the object. Internal forces don't count. This can be likened to a person sitting in an automobile and pushing against the dashboard. It doesn't matter how hard you push, you will have no effect on the speed of the automobile. This is because these forces are internal and act and react within the automobile itself. If no external force is present, then no change in speed is possible. A relaxed strike will hurt more than a strike that is tense, because a relaxed strike is allowed to sink into the target (with minimum time of contact), and use the target to aid in the reversal of direction (an outside force), and not its own muscles (inside force).

The same principle can be used to reverse direction and increase power in spinning techniques. Upon landing the spinning back fist, Benny "The Jet's" body is like a spring unwinding into a second spinning back fist with the other hand. Two things are occurring here: First, "The Jet" uses the necessity to reset his body into a fighting stance to launch a second attack. Second, he gains power in the spinning back fist by reversing direction upon impact.

Benny "The Jet" throws a double spinning back fist against Igari. Note how he utilizes the back of his hand and how his elbow is angled slightly downward. This strike would not be quite as powerful as the spinning back fist that utilizes the side of the hand (see pg. 62).
(From the archives of Pro-Action Publishing)

There is a difference between throwing two single strikes and throwing a two-strike combination. In a combination, you utilize the movement of the first strike to start the movement of the second strike. In other words, your strikes are helping one another. This is also a way to conserve energy. The shorter the movement, or the less time between strikes, the more energy is conserved, and you will last longer during heavy physical exertion. As mentioned earlier, because of less inertia (resistance to change), it is easier to keep a combination going than to start and stop many single strikes.

Impulse When Kicking

When kicking, the moment of impact must also be as short as possible, or the kick will result in a push, with the power dispersed into the target over a greater period of time. After the kick has landed, a quick reversal of the momentum will also result in an increase in power. To make the moment of impact as brief as possible, you must retrieve the kicking leg as fast as possible. This is accomplished by letting your foot "bounce" off your target.

When throwing a kick, then, you should rely on the following principles:

- Raise your leg in the cocked position. A common mistake is to raise the leg already straight, or almost straight. If the leg is straight, you will have difficulty accelerating the kick. This is especially true if the kick employs circular motion (round house kick, spinning back kick), because the rotational inertia will be greater. Raising your knee high may also help you rotate your hips easier. In addition, it keeps you better protected against your opponent's counter-blows.

- As you extend your leg to kick, you should think of impact as coming slightly before your leg is fully extended. This allows you to extend fully and through the target, allowing you to send the energy of the kick beyond the surface.

- Snap your leg back to the cocked position. The snap should come mainly from your opponent's body and not from the muscular control in your kick, thus creating a greater impulse by reversing the momentum. Make sure that your leg is snapped back in the same direction it originated from, or the greatest change in momentum cannot take place.

Note: Lifting your leg off the ground (cocking it), and throwing the kick may seem like two separate moves, but they need to be synchronized into one fluid motion, where there is no stop and restart of momentum.

Three Types of Impact

Successful fighting relies not only on the martial artist's ability to throw a powerful strike, but also on his ability to develop, understand, and use sound strategy. Every move should have a clear purpose of either set-up, knock-out or breaking, or positioning and balance. World champion kickboxer Benny "The Jet" Urquidez has recongnized three types of impact:

1. Stinging impact.
2. Shattering impact.
3. Breaking impact (which I will call "pushing impact" for consistency with previously discussed principles of physics).

Let's look at stinging impact first. Depending on what you wish to achieve, it is not always wise to produce a blow at its maximum force. You will therefore be better off developing a strategy that will earn you as many points as possible. This is done through a series of set-up moves. When you have created an opening in your opponent's defense, you can now strike with a quick but non-damaging blow. According to the Principle Of Impulse, the shorter the time the strike is in contact with the target, the greater the force. But in a point sparring match, the force will be low regardless of time, because the fighter uses his muscles (inside force) to "hold back" the power and to reverse the direction of the strike (see section on Reversing Direction By "Bouncing" pg. 75) This type of strike is likely to sting, but unlikely to do any significant damage. A strike with stinging impact is also useful as a strategic move to irritate your opponent, create openings, and split your opponent's focus prior to throwing a powerful knock-out punch in a full-contact match.

As demonstrated by Mike Stone, strikes with stinging impact are useful in karate point sparring competitions
(From the archives of Pro-Action Publishing, photo by Joe Griffith)

Shattering impact, on the other hand, is used to shock the body, as when delivering a knock-out strike or when breaking bones. Shattering impact is also used in board and brick breaking demonstrations. In this type of impact, the striking weapon should be in contact with the target a very short period of time, yet the practitioner must use extreme care not to rely on his muscles (inside force) to snap the strike back to the point of origin. There is a fine line here: in both the stinging impact and the shattering impact, the strike is very quick and "snappy". But the shattering impact has more power. Why? Because the strike is thrown relaxed and relies on the target to aid in the reversal of direction. This type of strike does not take a lot of muscular effort, yet it is very powerful and damaging. The practitioner must understand that powerful strikes must be snappy with a short time of contact, but not so snappy that the strike is starved by using muscular control to stop it and reverse its direction, as this would interfere with proper target penetration. A strike with shattering impact should rely on the target (outside force) to stop the strike and then, in effect, throw it back again (bouncing). The force is increased because the Impulse (change in momentum) is doubled when the strike reverse direction on impact.

This is an example from Nasty Anderson of a breaking or pushing impact. This is good when you want to reposition you opponent for a follow up technique.
(From the archives of Pro-Action Publishing)

Yoel Judah slips Ray Kleckner's left. Judah times his own right cross to connect as Kleckner is in a forward motion making his inertia impossible to stop. This is also an example of a shattering impact. The head moves, but the body remains planted. This is a perfect example of momentum and kinetic energy.
(From the archives of Pro-Action Publishing, photo by Danny Drake)

"Bouncing" occurs with shattering impact only, but it is not always obvious. Let's say for example, that you want to knock out your opponent with a punch to the jaw. But because the head is lighter than the body, and the neck is an inherently weak part of our anatomy, the strike is likely to continue through th target, rather than reversing direction on impact. The head will move, but the body will be "left behind". This is because of the inertia of the much heavier body. So, now you have both momentum which creates wallop, and kinetic energy which does damage. If you wanted to break a rib on the other hand, you can again use shattering impact. The shorter the time of contact, and the faster you reverse the direction of the strike (change the momentum), the more damaging the strike will be. Note: You don't have to have a "bounce" (only a short time of contact) with shattering impact, but if you do the force will increase.

Pushing impact is useful when you wish to reposition your opponent for follow-up attack. This type of impact keeps your striking weapon in contact with the target longer, and allows you to move (push) your opponent back against a wall or the ropes of the ring. Pushing impact works best if your opponent (the target) has somewhere to go. If your opponent is already up against a wall, pushing impact is difficult to use, as well as strategically unsound. If the target has no place to go, the time it takes for the strike to come to a stop will automatically be reduced, and shattering impact will result.

A push is not always obvious, as there are different degrees of pushing. A push does not have take a long time; only longer than a strike thrown with shattering impact. Pushing impact is great for stealing balance, especially when your opponent's base is narrow (as when he is in the process of throwing a kick). You can achieve pushing impact with a punch. But a strong kick, like a side thrust kick or front thrust kick, is better. Pushing impact can also be used in a takedown/grappling situation, as when you tackle your opponent preparatory to a takedown.

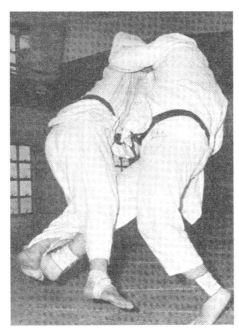

As demonstrated by Gene LeBell, tripping your opponent in conjunction with pushing impact is especially useful when attempting a takedown.
(From the archives of Pro-Action Publishing)

When executing a technique with pushing impact, you should focus on carrying the momentum through the target. This is why a stepping side thrust kick from long range is so effective, it allows you to build momentum, and to keep that momentum going until you have achieved the results of moving your opponent back. Depending on how dynamic your attack is, and because the human body is only capable of absorbing a certain amount of force, a technique using pushing impact may produce damage in addition to moving your opponent back. But this is outside of the principles of physics, and has more to do with human anatomy.

Penetrating the target is important in shattering impact as well, but rather, it is the energy that penetrates, and not the striking weapon itself. When breaking boards or bricks, as will be discussed in a later chapter, shattering impact is used. The bricks will break easiest if the time of contact is as short as possible, and if the striking weapon is made to reverse direction on impact.

To sum it up, it can be said that:

- The force can be increased by decreasing the time of contact, or by increasing the change in momentum (the impulse)

- Stinging impact is not really related to the physics of power, although it does have a valid strategic purpose

- Shattering impact has a lot of kinetic energy that goes through the target. Shattering impact is therefore the "deepest" of the three types of impact, and the most damaging.

- Pushing impact has a lot of momentum, and is useful both as a strategic move, as when unbalancing your opponent, and a power move as when keeping your opponent at long range with a kick.

- There is a fine line between the three types of impact. Unless you also practice, develop,and apply sound strategy, simply understanding the physics is not going to make you a master martial artist.

Impulse Exercise

Definition: Impulse is the change in momentum, which is also the product of the force acting on an object and the time during which it acts. We will give the force the letter "F", and the time the letter "t". Therefore, the Impulse = Ft. Or we can say that the change in momentum = force X time.

To change the momentum of an object, both the force and the time during which the force acts on the object are important. If you throw a punch, the force required to stop the punch will be smaller if it takes a long time to stop the punch, than if the punch is stopped quickly. Which hurts more, to hit a focus mitt that is soft, or to hit a granite slab? Slamming your knuckles into a granite slab is obviously going to hurt more. Why? Because the granite doesn't have "give", and the amount of time required to stop the punch is very small in comparison to hitting the focus mitt, which has "give" and allows your hand to sink into it gradually. When the time required to stop a punch is small, as in the case with the granite slab, the force will be large and will therefore hurt more.

Since the change in momentum = force X time, if you want to change the momentum of an object moving at a certain speed and coming to a complete stop, (as is the case when throwing a punch), a long time is compensated for by a small force, and a short time is compensated for by a large force.

When we say that one thing is equal to another, we call that an equation. Let's look at the equation change in momentum = force X time. For simplicity, I will choose some numbers that are easy to work with. If I give the force the number 5 and the time the number 2, then what would the change in momentum be? The equation would read change in momentum = 5 X 2, so the change in momentum would be 10, right? Why? Because 5 X 2 = 10.

Now, let's say that you are throwing a punch with a momentum of 10. In order to stop that punch, we would have to figure out the difference between 10 and 0 (which is when the punch comes to rest). The difference between 10 and 0 is 10, right? So, we could say that the change in momentum is 10. In the previous example, I chose the number 2 for the time. If I were to decrease the time to 1, then how much force would it take to stop the punch? Well, let's see, the equation says that the change in momentum = force X time, or 10 = something X 1. That "something" is the force. What number would you have to time 1 with to get 10? Answer: 10, of course! So, by comparing these two examples, we can see that by cutting the time of the impact (or the time it takes to stop the punch) in half, we also double the force. (The time went from a 2 to a 1, and the force went from a 5 to a 10). Are you with me so far?

So, in order to increase the force and make the punch more powerful, we have to decrease the time of impact. Another way to increase the force is to increase the change in momentum. Let's say that the change in momentum is 10, since the momentum went from a 10 to a 0, as in the example above. Now, let's say that the momentum goes from 10 to 0 and then back to 10 again, as would be the case if you threw a punch, let it come to a complete stop as it hit the target, and then let the target "throw it back again" in the same direction it came from (snapping the punch). Now, the change in momentum would be 20 instead of 10, since 10 to 0 and back to 10 again is equal to 20. Well, 20 is twice as large as 10, right? Let's say that the time of impact is still 1, then how large would the force be? Let's plug these numbers into the equation and see what happens.

Change in momentum = force X time. 20 = something X 1. The "something" is your force. The "something" must be equal to 20 in order to balance the equation. So, we can see that by snapping the punch back in the same direction it came from and with the same speed, we can double the force (we went from 10 to 20) and make the punch twice as powerful. Simple, eh?

Impulse Quiz

1. What is meant by striking "through" the target, and how is it accomplished?

Striking "through" means allowing the power of the strike to extend beyond the physical surface. Striking through the target can be accomplished by relaxing your muscles to allow full extension of the strike, and avoiding to subconsciously stop the strike short or pull it back too soon.

2. What is snap? In what way is it beneficial? What is the danger associated with snapping back too soon?

A strike that is "snappy" utilizes minimum time of contact with the target. The benefit of throwing a snappy strike is that the time the strike is in contact with the target is decreased, and therefore the force is increased. The opposite of snapping is "pushing". When you push, you allow your hand or foot to stay in contact longer, and power is reduced because the time is increased. We should strive toward throwing our strikes with snap, but there is a danger associated with snapping back too soon. A strike that is too "snappy" usually utilizes muscular control to reverse its direction, and therefore interferes with proper target penetration.

3. Why is power reduced when the time it takes to bring something to a stop is increased?

Impulse = change in momentum, which is also equal to force X time. When the momentum changes in a long period of time, the force (power) must decrease in order to balance the equation.

4. How can a martial artist taking a fall keep from getting hurt?

Many martial arts employ throwing techniques. It is therefore important to learn how to fall properly without risking injury. When the shock is absorbed gradually over a long period of time, the force is reduced and injury is less likely. This is accomplished by sequentially touching as many parts of your body to the floor as possible. A common example of this would be the forward roll, in which you absorb the impact through your hand, forearm, and shoulder. Your head, which is especially sensitive to injury, never touches the ground.

5. Why is the impulse increased in a strike that is made to bounce upon impact?

Impulse = change in momentum. When a strike comes to a stop upon impact, the momentum is changed to zero in a specific period of time. When a strike reverses direction, the momentum is again changed, and therefore the total change in momentum is greater than if the strike was simply brought to a stop. Bouncing aids in the reversal of direction, and therefore in the total change in momentum.

6. To enhance power, bouncing or "snap" must come from the target (externally), and not from the practitioner's muscular control (internally). Why?

Using muscular control to reverse direction would be equivalent to sitting in a car and pushing against the dashboard in an attempt to move the car forward. We can also think of this in terms of Newton's Third Law Of Motion (to every action there is an equal and opposite reaction). When you hit something, it hits you back. A strike should be thrown relaxed and with full extension (penetration), and allow the target to "throw the strike back" again.

Glossary

Equation-A term frequently used in math and physics to indicate that one thing is equal to another.

Force-Any influence that can cause an object to be accelerated.

Impulse-Change in momentum, or the force times the time interval. The shorter the time, the greater the force, and vice versa.

Inertia-Resistance to change in motion. An object at rest tends to stay at rest; an object in motion tends to stay in motion.

Kinetic Energy-Energy in motion (as opposed to potential energy). Kinetic energy is equal to one half the mass times the velocity squared. In chapter seven we will learn, in more detail, how this affects power.

Mass-The quantity of matter in an object. When acted upon by gravity, we can use mass interchangeably with weight.

Momentum-The product of the mass of an object and its velocity. The heavier the object, and the faster it travels, the greater the momentum.

Pounds Per Square Inch-The narrower the base of an object, the more pounds per square inch. A narrow base will be less stable than a wide base, but it will also have more penetrating capability. When falling, spreading your weight over as large an area as possible, will decrease the force.

Squared - A number times itself

Velocity-A measure of the speed of an object and its direction.

CHAPTER 6
Conservation Of Energy

The Workload

> **I like to fight when I'm really tired. Why? Because you can fight well when you're tired. You also know that you can pull that little extra out of you when needed, and still survive.**

It has been said that with sufficient stamina, you can wear down the most powerful adversary. Those of us who have competed, especially in a full-contact match, know to its fullest extent what it means to get tired. When you get tired, your years of training go out the door. Your techniques become worthless. Your power is reduced to zero. A blow, which you would ordinarily not have thought twice about, now makes you stagger across the ring close to a knock-out. Your legs are shaky. You struggle to maintain your balance. Your will to fight is reduced to the point that you might even take a technical knock-out willingly, just to get out of it.

Through my own experience, I'd like to say that the single most important factor in winning a fight is to keep from getting tired. Even now, years later, I remember the intense frustration in my first kick-boxing match. When I got back to my corner after the first round, I was so tired I didn't think it would be possible to get back out for the second round, let alone to fight! Close to the end of the third round, my opponent was so tired that she was up against the ropes, back on her heels, both hands down by her waist. And the look on her face is still today, all these years later, etched in my memory. I could hear my instructor yell from my corner: "Your right, throw your right!" It was a free shot; she was wide open. It would have been a free shot, if only I hadn't been so tired. There was no way I could have mustered the strength to throw that right hand toward a possible knock-out.

In a later fight, I was badly overpowered, constantly knocked backwards by a very aggressive opponent. I chose to cover up, to keep my cool. When I got back to my corner after the first round, my corner told me that "you can't just stand there and take it! You've got to hit her back! She won this round!" But knowing from past experience, that failing to conserve energy will tire a fighter in seconds, to me this was a strategic move. I just hoped that she would tire before she beaten me to a pulp. I won this bout by a knock-out in the second round. When my opponent had exhausted her supply of energy, when her strikes had lost their sting, when her moves went into slow time and her hands dropped to her waist, I had only to unleash a couple of good right hands. And what enabled me to do that was the fact that I had conserved my energy while she had not. How then do you conserve energy? How do you keep from getting tired?

What Is Power?

It is energy that enables you to do work. If you have a lot of energy, you can do a lot of work. Work is defined as force times distance. W=fd. Work is the product of the component of force that acts in the direction of motion and the distance moved. Two things are of importance every time work is done:

- You must exert a force.

- Something must be moved by that force.

As an exercise in power, I first had one of my students throw rear leg round house kicks in rapid succession on a kicking shield. I then had him throw lead leg round house kicks in rapid succession. Even though he had been throwing rear leg kicks first, and he was already getting tired, he told me how much easier it was to throw the lead leg round house fast.

For a given force, you can use a shorter distance to do less work. Work takes energy, so if you can do as little work as possible and still attain a considerable amount of power, you will last longer during heavy physical exertion. Because work is the product of the force and the distance, if you can decrease the distance you can increase the force, and vice versa.

If you view Mike Tyson's hooking strategies, you will find that he has tremendous power. One of the reasons for this is that he uses short, explosive moves that employ a very short distance for the exertion of the force. By relying on the power in his body, he can sacrifice distance for a greater advantage. Again, this becomes a gain/lose situation. We have talked about how distance allows you to build momentum for a strong punch; that's why your rear techniques are often stronger than your lead techniques. Increasing the distance, however, also increases the WORKload. If you continuously throw your strikes from a long distance, more work is done, and more energy is needed, and you will get tired faster. "Short punching", in which the martial artist relies on the mass and explosiveness in his body, will help you conserve energy for a longer duration.

That which enables you to do work is energy. There is potential energy that is stored and held in readiness. Once released, this energy becomes kinetic energy (movement of mass), which we will look at in more detail in the next chapter. If you have a lot of energy, you can do a lot of work. Power is a measure of how fast the work is done. Power = work/time interval. Being twice as powerful as your opponent means that you can do the same amount of work in half the time, or twice the work in the same time. Consider how much more tired you get when doing something fast than when doing it slow. What about explosive power? Bruce Lee understood the concept of explosive power.

After my instructor had made me sprint up a hill five times to build explosiveness, he had the guts to tell me that I move like a buffalo!

So, why do you get more tired when running a mile than when walking it? Why do you get more tired when fighting aggressively, than when relying on defense and only exploding with an offensive technique when it is to your advantage to do so?

Bruce Lee's One-Inch Punch

One of the things that Bruce Lee was famous for was the one-inch punch. From what we have learned about power so far, the one-inch punch contradicts the principle of distance: the longer the distance, the more time you have to build momentum for power, which is also why boxers and kick-boxers fight with their stronger side farther away from their opponent.

Many years ago I heard about a martial artist of the Wing Chun system who could throw the one-inch punch. I looked him up and asked if he would demonstrate it to me. To my delight, he said he would. He handed me a phone book to hold against my chest for protection. He faced me, held his hand in the vertical position, and touched his finger tips to the phone book. He concentrated for a few seconds, then pulled his fingers back into a fist. The next thing I knew, I was with my back against the wall five feet behind me. I was still holding the phone book, but my whole body was tingling from his punch and from hitting the wall. I think that my feet must have become airborne. I have no recollection of them dragging across the floor. The Wing Chun stylist told me that the explosive power comes from the elbow.

Explosiveness means higher impulse; a very short time at the moment of impact, and therefore a lot of power. Explosiveness can offset the lack of distance. From what I observed of the one-inch punch, the Wing Chun stylist's elbow was bent prior to throwing the punch. It was also held in front of his body along his centerline. In addition, his hand was in the vertical position, which allowed him to keep his elbow down and use his body, which is heavier than the arm, to initiate the movement of the punch. I have since then experimented moderately with the one-inch punch and found that, even from a horse stance, you can attain considerable power by keeping your elbow in front of your body and pivoting your foot, hip, and shoulder in unison. The technique is to make the initial move explosive. Again, the shorter the time of impact, the more powerful the punch. If the punch results in a push, or anything that even slightly resembles it, from a short distance not much power can be attained.

To every action there is an equal and opposite reaction. When one object collides with another, the total momentum is conserved, but may be redistributed to the other object. Consider a fist (with the full weight of the body behind it) moving toward a person at rest. When the fist hits the person, the momentum is redistributed to the person, and the person is moved back. Momentum = mass X velocity.

So the question remains, does the one-inch punch really exist? Yes, it does. Can anybody do it? Not likely without a considerable amount of practice. Can a small person throw a powerful one-inch punch? Yes, but if his initial move is no faster than the heavier person's, then the heavier person's punch will have more power than the lightweight's.

Simply knowing the principles of physics will not make you a great martial artist. It still takes years of training to get your body mechanics correct, so that you can utilize these principles to their fullest. I think the way to start to learn the one-inch punch is to work on synchronizing your moves, so they work in unison.

Conservation Of Energy

There are many ways in which you can conserve energy throughout a fight. One is by relying on defense while your opponent is relying on offense. Not being hit, such as with a slip; a bob and weave; and a feint are among the best ways to conserve energy. Another way is to use your opponent's movement to your advantage. The less you have to move, the more energy you will conserve. This becomes especially important when in a confined area, such as a ring used in boxing or kick-boxing. Even in a street encounter, you will usually be in a confined area.

When you get really tired, something as simple as taking a step forward may seem difficult. But since your forward movement adds momentum to your techniques and therefore power, you don't want to sacrifice this movement entirely. This is where timing becomes important. If you can time your strikes, create maximum impact at the time of contact, you will be able to gain considerable momentum. Simultaneously, you will conserve your own energy by minimizing your own movement.

Blocks are effective defensive tools against strikes or kicks. However, when you use a block to defend against an attack, you will momentarily tie up the blocking weapon, making you unable to use it again until defense is complete. If you can rely on movement where you are not hit as mentioned above, you will leave your hands and feet free for offense. In other words, you can use defense and offense simultaneously, which will speed up the fight giving you the advantage. While your opponent is still thinking of offense, you are already landing your next strike, while at the same time having successfully defended against his attack. However, you should only anticipate, but never rely on your opponent's game plan. Your strategy should be fluid.

If your opponent is in the habit of throwing leg kicks, you can anticipate such a kick, or even draw it from him by "giving" him your leg. Right before the kick connects, instead of blocking it, use the momentum and energy of your opponent's attack to launch a counter-attack.

This photo sequence shows Benny "The Jet" conserving energy by going with the motion of his opponent's kick, creating offense by bringing maximum power with least effort.
(From the archives of Pro-Action Publishing)

If the blocking leg has "give", you can go with the motion. The power is then redistributed over a longer time, and the impact will not be felt as much (concept of impulse). Note how Benny "The Jet" allows his leg to bend and go with the motion of his opponent's kick. Because his opponent is on one leg and in the process of kicking, he is also unable to move away until his kick is complete. By utilizing the momentum of your opponent's kick to set your own kick in motion, you will have accomplished three things: defended against the attack; conserved your energy; and come back with offense when your opponent is the most vulnerable. Benny "The Jet" calls this defense "coil and recoil."

In kick-boxing, energy can be conserved whenever you can dominate the center of the ring. This means very small movements on your part, while your opponent will be forced to move around you in big circles. Conservation of energy during a fight that is lengthy may be crucial to winning. In addition, when your opponent is cornered and you only give him one way to get out, he has to take that route. This makes fighting somewhat predictable. If you know beforehand which way your opponent is going to move through testing his reations, you can launch an attack in that direction and land it with certainty.

In the pictures below, "The Jet's" opponent, Kunimatsu Okao, is on the ropes. If he continues in the direction he has already started towards The Jet's left, a good technique would be the spinning back kick, because the kick can be thrown with less than 180 degrees of turn. Okao will be walking into the power of the kick, the kick will land with certainty, and energy is conserved by utilizing as little movement as possible.

Benny "The Jet" conserves energy by placing his opponent, Kunimatsu Okao, against the ropes and giving Okao only one way to escape; to Okao's right (the corner is to the left).
(From the archives of Pro Action Publishing)

Okao moves to his right. Benny "The Jet" throws a round house kick off of his lead leg. This is the quickest technique because this is the leg closest to the target. This is a very hard impact because Okao is moving into the technique. This move uses the least energy because it has the shortest distance to travel.
(From the archives of Pro Action Publishing)

Okao moves to his left. Benny "The Jet" has to spin less than 180 degrees with a spinning back kick.
(From the archives of Pro Action Publishing)

Using The Spinning Back Kick Strategically

Because a fight is constantly dynamic, your opponent will seldom stand in one place and allow you to bombard him with punches and kicks. In order to land a technique with power, you must adjust to your opponent's movement. This is perhaps especially important when throwing a technique that is lengthy (takes more time than other techniques), or one that requires you to turn your back toward your opponent. The reason that the spinning back kick is difficult to land is because we fail to adjust to our opponent's movement.

If both you and your opponent are in left fighting stances, the best time to throw the spinning back kick is when your opponent is moving to his right (your left). This will enable you to throw the kick with less than 180 degrees of turn. In other words, your opponent will be "walking into the kick" (economy of motion). Throwing a kick which your opponent meets halfway will be more economical than having to "chase" your opponent with the kick. Landing the spinning back kick when your opponent is moving to his left (your right) is more difficult, because you will need to spin more than 180 degrees.

$$\boxed{\begin{array}{c} \text{Work = force x distance} \\ \text{or} \\ \text{W= Fd} \end{array}}$$

Work = **F**d

When your opponent moves to his right, you can land the spinning back kick with less than 180 degrees of turn. Your opponent will be "walking into" your kick.

Work = F**d**

When your opponent moves to his left, you will need to spin more than 180 degrees. You will be "chasing" your opponent with the kick.

Caution: Your opponent is more likely to move to his left than to his right, because it is easier to step with the lead leg laterally from a left fighting stance than it is to step right from a left fighting stance. You must therefore train for your opponent's lateral movement to his left (your right). If your opponent fights with his lead leg right then the opposite is true.

The concept of adjusting to your opponent's lateral movement can be likened to shooting a bird in flight (from a perpendicular angle). Since you know that the bird is moving forward, and you know that it will take some time for the bullet to reach the bird after you pull the trigger, you must aim slightly in front of the bird.

When shooting a bird in flight, you must aim where the bird is going to be when the bullet reaches it. This is called "timing".

When throwing the spinning back kick against an opponent moving to your right, you must aim your kick where he is going to be when the kick lands, and not where he is at the initiation of the kick.

The spinning back kick can be thrown at many different stages during the fight:

- As a follow-up off another strike or kick.

- As defense against an aggressive fighter coming toward you.

- As a strategic move to keep your opponent on the ropes.

Because we know that it is easier and more economical to throw the spinning back kick against an opponent who is moving to your left (if in a left fighting stance), by being strategically smart, you can now "lure" your opponent into moving to your left. A good time to do this is when your opponent is on the ropes.

Being on the ropes is usually a position of weakness, and your opponent will look for an escape path. By cutting off his escape path to his left, his only way out will be to his right. Now, when you can anticipate his move, you can throw the spinning back kick when he starts moving to his right. Landing the spinning back kick at this time is almost a given. Because your opponent will be moving toward the kick and into its path of power, the kick will land regardless of how far your opponent has stepped when you throw it.

Energy Quiz

1. How can you keep from getting tired when fighting?

Even if you are in very good shape, if the fight is lengthy, it is almost impossible to keep from getting tired. A fighter can last longer during heavy physical exertion if he learns how to conserve energy throughout the course of the fight.

2. Name a few ways in which you can conserve energy.

Energy can be conserved by shortening the movement required to execute a technique. For example, use short explosive moves that rely on the power in your body. Or get your opponent to expend more energy than you by dominating the center of the fight and making him move around you. When you get tired, rely on defense until you have recuperated enough to come back with good offense. A fighter who is very tired, yet tries to rely on offense, will lose the sting in his strikes, and the strikes will not do any damage.

3. Some of the principles of physics behind power seem contradictory and often rely on a "gain/lose" situation, where sometimes you will need to give something up in order to gain a greater advantage. Explain how distance can work to either your advantage or disadvantage.

The longer the distance, the more time you have to build momentum. That is why your rear techniques often seem stronger than your lead techniques. This is where a longer distance will work to your advantage. Increasing the distance also increases the workload. When more work is done, more energy is needed, and you will get tired faster.

4. What is the main advantage of power?

The main advantage of power is the acceleration it can produce. In turn acceleration translates into more devastating strikes.

5. In regards to power, when is the best time to throw the spinning back kick and why?

The best time to throw the spinning back kick is when your opponent is moving toward its path of power. The spinning back kick relies on circular movement, and because a fight often moves circular, you should strive toward throwing the kick whenever your opponent moves in a direction that enables you to spin less than 180 degrees. This will help you conserve energy, and will take less time because less movement is needed.

6. How can you use the spinning back kick as a strategic move, forcing your opponent to move into its path of power?

If both you and your opponent are in left fighting stances, you know that your opponent will favor moving to your right (his left), because his left foot will be forward, thus making it easier to step with that foot first (the opposite is true if you are both in right fighting stances). Because you can conserve more energy in the spinning back kick if your opponent moves to your left, you should use the spinning back kick strategically against an opponent on the ropes by cutting off his escape path to your right, thereby forcing him to move to your left.

Glossary

Energy-That which enables you to do work. If you have a lot of energy, you can do a lot of work.

Force-Any influence that can cause an object to be accelerated.

Impulse-Change in momentum, or the force times the time interval. The shorter the time, the greater the force, and vice versa.

Kinetic Energy-Half the mass times the speed squared. Kinetic energy depends on the mass and speed of the object. If a fighter can double his speed, he can quadruple his kinetic energy. Kinetic energy has a great capability of doing damage.

Mass-The quantity of matter in an object. When acted upon by gravity, we can use mass interchangeably with weight.

Momentum-The product of the mass of an object and its velocity. The heavier the object, and the faster it travels, the greater the momentum.

Potential Energy-Energy that is stored and held in readiness. Once released, it becomes kinetic energy.

Power-In physics, power is equal to work divided by time interval. Cutting the time interval enables you to attain more power. The martial artist often thinks of power in terms of how much damage one is able to do when landing a strike.

Squared - A number times itself

Velocity--A measure of the speed of an object and its direction.

Work-Force times distance. For a given force, you can use a shorter distance to do less work. Work takes energy, so if you can do as little work as possible, you can attain a considerable amount of power.

CHAPTER 7
Ki-netic Energy

Mind Over Matter

Fact: You will get hit some time during your martial arts career. Knowing this in advance, which fighter would you rather take a punch from? The big fat one, or the small skinny one?

From what we have learned about body mass in motion, it would seem logical to choose the small fighter over the big one. But because power is a combination of many factors, including momentum, distance, speed, acceleration, inertia, and energy, there will often be a give/take situation, where sometimes one of these factors is decreased in order to increase another. Consider inertia, for example. Inertia means resistance to change. This also means that once an object is set in motion, it becomes difficult to stop it or to change its direction. But it is also difficult to set the object in motion in the first place. The more mass, the more inertia. A heavy fighter must therefore expend more energy to set himself in motion than does a lightweight.

Because force is a combination of mass and acceleration, F=ma, we can assume that it hurts more to get hit by a heavy fighter who has the mass of his body behind his strikes. But this is true only if this fighter also has the ability to accelerate as fast as a lightweight. It is interesting to note that it hurts more to get hit by a fast moving lightweight than it does to get hit by a slow moving heavyweight. Why? Because a light fighter moving with the same momentum as the heavyweight has more kinetic energy.

You cannot strike somebody effectively without setting your fist (or striking weapon) in motion. Energy of motion is called kinetic energy. Kinetic energy depends on the mass and speed of the object. We already know that the more mass, the more capable you are of producing a powerful strike. We also know that the higher the speed, the more capable you are of producing a powerful strike.

Note: A fast moving heavyweight can produce more power than an equally fast moving lightweight, because the heavyweight has more momentum. But fast moving heavyweights are not often seen. Because of inertia, it takes more energy to set a heavyweight into motion than a lightweight. When you expend more energy, you get tired quicker. And when you get tired, your strikes will lose their sting.

The Power Paradox

The interesting point about kinetic energy is that it is equal to half the mass multiplied by the square of the speed. Kinetic energy = 1/2 mass times the speed squared. A light fighter who is only half as massive as a heavy fighter, but who is moving with the same momentum, will have twice the velocity (speed). But in the kinetic energy equation the speed is squared. If the speed of an object is doubled, its kinetic energy is quadrupled, and the object can do four times as much work at only twice the speed. An object moving twice as fast as another takes four times as much work to stop. Faster speed = more kinetic energy by the square (not proportional). While momentum is proportional to velocity, kinetic energy is proportional to the square of velocity. An object that moves with twice the velocity of another object of the same mass has twice the momentum, but four times the kinetic energy. It can provide twice the impulse, but do four times as much work. The object will penetrate four times as far. It will deliver four times the damage!

Speed in fighting now becomes extremely important. Twice the velocity will give you four times the energy. If a fighter is only half as massive as his opponent, however, twice the velocity won't give him four times the energy, because his mass is half, but it will give him twice the kinetic energy. It takes more effort to move a heavy fighter, so which is best: a heavy fighter with a lot of momentum, or a lighter fighter with a lot of kinetic energy? This is where your speed will offset your opponent's weight, and being a lightweight can actually give you the advantage power wise.

Consider throwing a side thrust kick. The side thrust kick is one of the more powerful kicks, which is often used to keep an aggressive opponent at a distance.

Joe Lewis (left) executes one of his patented side kicks which raises Byong Yu off the ground.
(From the archives of Pro-Action Publishing)

When the kick connects, the momentum is transferred from your body to your opponent's. If you can speed up the kick so that it strikes with twice the speed, you will be able to knock your opponent twice as far. Or if you can time the kick so that your opponent steps forward into it, you will add his momentum to that of your kick, and the kick will knock him farther than if you rely solely on your own momentum. So, by increasing the momentum, you will increase the impulse, because the change in momentum, as your foot comes to a stop, will be greater.

A side thrust kick thrown twice as fast has twice the impulse, but it has four times the kinetic energy, and will penetrate four times as far and do four times the damage! Increasing the speed increases the impulse proportionally, but the kinetic energy is increased by the square. The speed of a lightweight fighter has a great capability of generating damage. The heavyweight, who is twice as heavy as you, will be able to generate twice the momentum and twice the impulse. But if you can increase your speed to twice that of the heavyweight, you will not be able to do equal damage to him as one might think, but twice the damage! If you can rely on "bouncing" (reversal of motion), you will increase the impulse and do even more damage. If the kick can bounce (be thrown back) elastically with no loss in speed, the change in momentum and impulse is doubled. See the chapter on Impulse.

You can win a fight by using momentum to your advantage. Increase momentum by increasing speed, and by keeping the weight of your body behind all strikes. But if the product of your opponent's mass and velocity matches yours, however, you will be stopped short. The jarring exerted from the combined momentum of you and your opponent will be the same.

Being able to stop a fighter from pushing you back against the ropes is one thing, but what about doing damage? Again, if you are the lightweight, and you can move faster than your opponent who is the heavyweight, you will do more damage, you will hurt him more, because a light fighter moving with the same momentum has more kinetic energy. Instead of trying to gain weight for an upcoming fight, try to gain speed.

How Important Is Kinetic Energy?

Kinetic energy is energy in motion with penetrating capabilities. If I were to tell you that a punch has more momentum than a bullet, would you believe me? The heavier something is, the greater the momentum. One of the best examples of this is a cruise ship. Because of its enormous size, the captain has to turn the engines off a mile or more from shore, or he would be unable to bring the ship to a stop. Your fist might weigh 20 times more than a bullet, so the momentum of your fist would be great compared to the bullet, even at a slower speed. But the kinetic energy of the bullet will offset the advantages of more momentum. Let's figure this out:

$$\text{Momentum} = \text{mass (weight)} \times \text{velocity (speed)}$$
$$\text{Kinetic Energy} = 1/2 \text{ mass} \times \text{velocity squared}$$

Let's say that the mass of the fist is 2 kg (for simplicity). The speed of the fist is 3 meters/second (for simplicity). Using the momentum equation above, the momentum of the fist would be 2 X 3 = 6.

Let's say that the mass of the bullet is 0.01 kg. The speed of the bullet is 200 meters/second. Using the momentum equation above, the momentum of the bullet would be 0.01 X 200 = 2.

So, the fist has more momentum than the bullet. You can knock somebody over with your fist, but the bullet is not likely to knock a person to the ground. The bullet is more likely to penetrate the person's body. Let's see how much kinetic energy the bullet has.

$$\text{KE (fist)} = 2/2 \times 3 \text{ squared} = 1 \times 9 = 9.$$
$$\text{KE (bullet)} = 0.01/2 \times 200 \text{ squared} = 0.005 \times 40000 = 200.$$

The ratio of kinetic energy between the bullet and the fist is 200/9 = 22.22.

The bullet has 22.22 times the kinetic energy of the heavier fist, and is 22.22 times more likely to do penetrating damage! These numbers are not scientific. I just used numbers that seemed reasonable and were easy to work with. However, if the numbers I used really represented the actual weights and speeds of the fist and bullet, the result would be scientific and is proven through the equation. The point is that unless your goal is to knock somebody over, or to lay on top of him and crush him, weight is not necessarily that important, speed is.

The first picture on the following page shows a martial artist sending kinetic energy down through a stack of bricks. Kinetic energy however, does not travel through air easily, because the air molecules would use the path of least resistance and disperse to the sides. It is therefore not possible to strike a person from across the room without touching him.

The second picture on the next page shows the practitioner breaking a stack of ice. But since the blocks of ice are separated with space, he could not choose to break the bottom block only, while leaving the top ones intact. Unless the top block breaks and touches the one below it, the energy does not have a medium to travel through.

"Jaco" shutos breaking through 11 cynder blocks.
(From the archives of Pro-Action Publishing, photo by Mary Townsley)

John J. Williams breaking a stack of ice.
(From the archives of Pro-Action Publishing)

Why is there space between the blocks of ice and concrete blocks? When breaking a pile of bricks and there is space between each brick, you only need to exert a force that is a little larger than what it takes to break one brick. When this brick collapses on the one below it, momentum and energy is transferred down through the pile. A small amount of the force is also lost due to friction and heat.

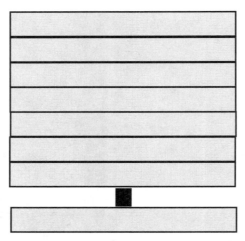

Is it possible to choose, for example, the last block to be broken in a stack while leaving the others undamaged? Yes, it is possible to send kinetic energy through a stack of bricks and break only the one on the bottom while leaving the others intact. However, the bricks must be touching each other and energy must have a medium to travel through.

Here is a stack of eight bricks. The top seven bricks are resting on one another. The one on the bottom is separated from the others by a layer of air. However, there is a small peg leading from the top stack to the brick on the bottom. If the karate practitioner can strike the top of the pile with enough force to break one brick only, the energy will transfer through the pile, then through the peg, and down to the bottom brick, which will break. The top seven bricks will not break because they are acting as a unit, and there is not enough power in the practitioner's strike to break the whole unit. If there was no peg (only air) between the unit and the bottom brick, the energy would not have a medium to travel through, and it would not be possible to break the brick on the bottom.

A bullet can penetrate a target easier than a fist, not only because of the speed and kinetic energy, but also because the force is focused over a very small surface area. In the picture below, Johnny Lee is seen bending steel rods that are pushed into his throat. Undoubtedly, being successful at this takes some tightening of the muscles in the throat, and also choosing an area of the throat that is less sensitive to damage (probably not the Adam's apple).

When initiating this exercise, the rods should be placed at a slight diagonal angle upward against the throat and not straight into it. This allows the practitioner to spread the force over a larger surface area. Once the rods have started to bend, a weakness is created in the rods and focus can be maintained downward to finish the exercise. The principle that is used here is pounds per square inch (force per surface area).

Also ask yourself why the rods are so long? If the practitioner was using a foot long rod instead, would he still be able to do the exercise? The longer the rod, the more sag you get in the middle, which will assist you at bending the rod. If you can cause a slight vibration (a wave) in the rod, you will create what is called resonance. Hanging bridges have been caused to collapse because of resonance.

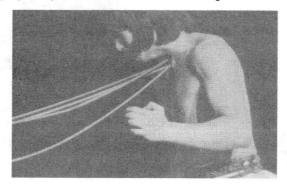

Johnny Lee is bending steel rods pushed into his throat.
[From the archives of Pro Action Publishing, photo by Frank Cohen]

Mind Over Matter

Breaking techniques are often demonstrated in karate tournaments. One of these techniques involves not the actual power of a person's fist or foot as it goes through the target, but the "internal power" of the practitioner as the object is broken against his body.

A stack of bricks on Joseph Jennings' chest is broken with a sledge hammer. The practitioner is resting on a bed of nails.
(From the archives of Pro-Action Publishing, photo by Warren Doering)

This is really a demonstration of the difference between momentum and kinetic energy. Remember, momentum only creates wallop (the ability to knock something over), while kinetic energy does damage (penetrates).

When the hammer is swung, it has both momentum and kinetic energy. The bricks break, but the martial artist who is resting on the bed of nails is not harmed. Yet, every bit of the momentum of the hammer goes into the artist's body. However, most of the kinetic energy never gets to him, but is absorbed into the breaking of the bricks. The energy that does remain is distributed over hundreds of nails. The force per surface area is not enough to penetrate the skin.

Try this same experiment lying on one nail only, and I guarantee that the results will be painfully different! Next time you witness this experiment, pay attention to how the practitioner is lowered and raised from the bed of nails. Most likely he will not sit and lie on it the way one would normally sit and lie on a bed. Instead he will have help from two or more fellow martial artists. This enables him to touch all the nails simultaneously, already from the beginning distributing the force over the whole area of his back, with no single nail given the "advantage" of the practitioner's whole weight.

And then there are those martial artists who walk barefoot on burning coal as part of a belt promotion. Yes, it takes a great deal of fortitude to overcome the fear of getting burned. But in reality, and if the martial artist knew something about physics, he would have little to fear. Walking barefoot on burning coal is possible not because of the martial artist's extensive training in overcoming pain, but because your feet are protected by natural perspiration, which creates an insulating layer between the coals and the skin of your feet. Nervousness before performing the feat is actually to your advantage, because nervousness causes more perspiration.

Have you ever extinguished a candle by wetting your fingers and squeezing the wick? Same principle.

So, what about this "mind over matter" type of fighting, where a martial artist claims to be able to strike somebody from across the room without being within reach to physically touch him? Does it really work?

I once tried to get this demonstrated, but was told that the energy was too great, and that it would have a very damaging effect on me. And because the "true" martial artists don't use their powers to hurt, but only in self-defense, the master was not willing to demonstrate his technique on me. So I asked if he would consider striking an object instead of a person, say for example, to knock a vase off a table? I was unsuccessful in this matter as well. Was told that the "object" has to be alive for it to work. Why? After a lot of thought on this matter, I came to the conclusion that it is in fact possible to strike a person from a distance without physically touching him, but only if that person knows in advance that he is going to get hit, hence why the object has to be alive; a dead object does not have the ability to know in advance. This theory works not on the actual powers of the master, but on the perceived powers of the master and on the anticipation of the person receiving the blow, and on the principle of "freezing".

Have you ever been in a full contact match where you know beforehand that you will get hit some time during the fight, and where you also know that you will get judged on your ability to take a good punch? In particular if your opponent has a reputation, this anticipation of the blow will often cause you to freeze (tense) whenever you think that you are going to get hit, even if your opponent does not throw an actual strike. For example, if you have already tasted some of his power and you know that it hurts, and therefore you respect it, or if you respect this person because of his reputation, he now simply needs to fake a strike to get you to tense. This tensing of the muscles often translates into pain, although it has no lasting effect.

Flash Knockout

There are some boxing matches where one of the fighters has been accused of going down with a "flash knockout". Some may even think that such matches are fixed, where the winner does not actually strike the opponent with a punch containing knockout power, but that he has been instructed to act as if he is getting knocked out. My belief is that those fighters who do get knocked out by a "flash knock-out" do so because of their fear and anticipation of the other fighter's power, and not because they were actually hit by a powerful strike. This is where the real mind over matter comes in, and where the skill of the master lies in intimidation rather than in **ki** or other physical principles. This is also why a fighter must know in advance that he is going to get hit. Lacking this knowledge would make him unable to fear the strike, and he would therefore not get tense in anticipation of it.

It is of course, possible to get knocked out by a powerful strike. But once you know that you are going to get hit, you must now train your mind to eliminate the fear factor or the desire to tense. When I start training with a new student, one of the exercises we do in the second or third lesson is getting used to seeing a punch coming at you. I put my boxing gloves on and have my student move with me, but without throwing anything. I will now randomly start flicking jabs toward the student's face, but without actually hitting him. Our natural reaction to this is to close our eyes and jerk our head back. After sufficient training, the student will learn to mentally tell himself not to close his eyes, but to stay focused on the opponent. Once you become used to the fight game and your confidence grows, you can use your own "powers" (your mental determination) to counteract your tendency to freeze. This is when the fighter, or master, who has relied on his reputation will be stripped, and this mind over matter fighting will no longer have an effect. Think of the Mike Tyson/Buster Douglas bout. Douglas, an inferior contender experienced his mother's death and his girlfriend in the hospital the week of his historic fight. His thoughts were not focused on the mighty Tyson, so he was able to give Iron Mike his first defeat via a knock out.

Other Incredible Physical Feats

As mentioned earlier, kinetic energy must have a medium to travel through. That's why it is not possible to break the bottom brick in the pile, unless that brick is connected somehow to the top bricks. That is also why it is not possible to strike somebody from across the room without being within reach to physically touch him. But what about air? Does air not qualify as a medium for the energy to travel through?

Air does qualify, but the problem is that air is a gas that is compressible. If possible, the air molecules will also disperse to the sides, taking the path of least resistance. For air to be used as a medium for kinetic energy, it must be compressed at a very fast rate. If a person stands at one end of the room and mentally focuses on hitting a person at the other end of the room, nothing will happen. If he throws a punch in the air toward the person at the other end of the room, again, nothing will happen. However, if you throw a punch that comes fast enough and close enough to the target, it is possible to move the hairs on your opponent's head without actually touching. If the air molecules can be compressed fast enough to exert pressure in the direction of the punch, it will be felt by your opponent. However, it will not hurt him, because the human body is not capable of generating a rate of compression that is fast enough to keep the air molecules from dispersing to the sides. A jet-engine, however, can generate a very strong and focused stream of air. I have personally seen a pickup truck rolled on its side, when the driver drove behind a running jet engine at a distance of over a hundred yards. All the windows in the truck were also shattered.

The picture below shows the great master Mas Oyama extinguishing a candle with his punch, but without actually touching the flame. When it comes to air and fire, an interesting thing occurs. Fire needs air in order to burn, and air will actually fuel the fire. Too much air however, will extinguish the flame. If Mas Oyama threw his fist slower and provided a gentler draft, the candle would burn more violently. But by using a great deal of speed and snap, the air molecules will hit the flame in greater number over shorter time, and the cooling effect is enough to extinguish the candle. If you were to extinguish a candle by blowing, which works best: blowing slowly and gently, or blowing forcefully in a quick spurt? If Mas Oyama's fist didn't get close enough to the candle, he wouldn't be able to extinguish it, because the air molecules would disperse to the sides. What Mas Oyama is doing takes both speed and distance awareness.

Mas Oyama extinguishes a candle with the snap of his punch.
(From the archives of Pro-Action Publishing)

The more massive an object, the more inertia it has. This means that if the object is in a state of motion, it will be difficult to stop it. It also means that if the object is in a state of rest, it will be difficult to set it in motion. In the picture below, Mas Oyama is seen cutting the top off of a freestanding bottle.

$$\boxed{\text{Kinetic energy} = 1/2 \text{ mass x velocity squared}}$$

Kinetic Energy = 1/2mV squared

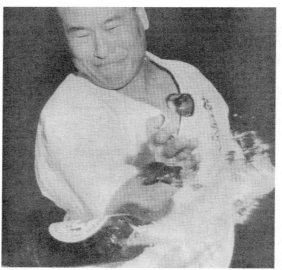

Mas Oyama cuts the top off of a free standing bottle with a shuto (knife hand strike).
(From the archives of Pro-Action Publishing)

Here, several things are occurring simultaneously:

- The bottle has a wider base than top. This means that the base is stable with a low center of gravity.

- Because of the size of the bottle and the liquid in it, the bottom is heavier than the top and therefore possesses a great deal of inertia. If the bottle was empty, it would need to be tied to the table or be held steady by someone.

- The speed with which the break occurs is important. More speed means more kinetic energy, and it is therefore possible (in this case, literally) to take the strike through the target.

- Because of the speed, there is more kinetic energy than momentum. Kinetic energy does damage, while momentum provides wallop. If the momentum was higher and the kinetic energy lower, the top would not be cut off the bottle, but the whole bottle would be knocked over instead.

- Mas Oyama is using a shuto (the knife side of his hand). This enables him to focus the energy over a small surface area, which in turn means more force per square inch. If he was using the whole palm of his hand instead, he would not be as likely to succeed.

Some martial artists give the appearance of "making themselves lighter" by walking on fragile objects without breaking them. But because we are acted upon by the same amount of gravity all the time, the only way you can make yourself lighter is by going on a diet and losing weight. However, a fragile object (a glass, for example) may become strong because of its structural shape. Why is the roof over an athletic arena dome shaped and not flat? You obviously can't have pillars in an athletic arena to support the weight of the roof, so a dome is built. The strength of a dome follows the same principles as the strength of an arch (the St. Louis Gateway Arch, for example, or a doorway arch which has to support the weight of the building without collapsing).

 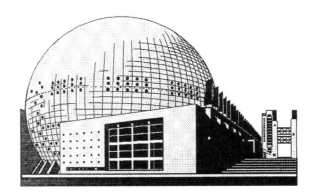

The strength of an arch or athletic dome lies in its structural shape.

A flat roof will sag in the middle. Take a sheet of paper and hold it horizontally in each end. Observe how the middle is sagging. Now apply pressure inward (towards the center) until the paper becomes arched upward. These inward forces compress the building materials, increasing the stability. You can even place an object of considerable weight on top of the arched paper without it sagging.

Another point to consider is how the force is distributed. Most people would agree that an egg is very fragile. But if you take an egg and make your hands conform to its shape, you will find that the egg is remarkably strong. Breaking the egg by squeezing your hands together while applying the pressure equally across the whole surface area of the egg, will make the egg difficult to break. If you put one finger on each end of the egg, however, and poke it, the force is focused over a very small surface area and will penetrate the egg easier. When you see a martial artist walk on a fragile object, I would bet that this object is probably dome shaped, and that the martial artist's foot is made to conform to the shape of the object, distributing the weight over a larger surface area.

There is one more thing, which is a bit outside of the physics of power, but which still needs to be said, and that is the capability of the human mind.

That lady was huge, man! And really mean looking, with U.S. Marine Corps tattooed on her arms. There was nothing at all that was lady-like about her. She knocked her opponent out in the first round. But I think that she won the fight by intimidation before it had even begun.

Imposing Your Will

Make your opponent fight your fight. This should be your foremost thought and strategy both during your fight preparation and during the actual contest. A stance for example, should be both offensive and defensive. Offensively, you must give your opponent a threat. Look confident and ready. Defensively, you must cover your openings. A stance can therefore be thought of as both mental and physical. Don't let your mind use its psychological powers to drain energy from you and slow your speed.

Benny "The Jet's" fighting stance.
(From the archives of Pro Action Publishing)

Note how Benny "The Jet's" legs are slightly bent to lower his center of gravity for stability. Yet, he is not rigid. He is not just standing there waiting to see what will happen. Through his stance, he has already taken charge of the fight. Note also how his rear foot is ready to push off against the floor for a quick forward shuffle. This "readiness" adds to the mental characteristics of the stance. It is obvious that "The Jet" can't wait to engage in battle.

It is interesting to me, especially with less experienced fighters, that they always seem to concentrate on their opponent's strengths. I often hear such comments as "I've heard he's got a great right hand" or "She's got legs from hell". This immediately tells me that your opponent has the advantage. Before a punch has even been thrown, you are already fighting his fight.

Now, tell me this, why would you want to concentrate on what your opponent does well? Instead, you should be stating those comments about yourself. I recall a particular fight where my fighter was new to the Thai-boxing rules, which allow for knee strikes, leg kicks, and elbows. I remember the concerns my fighter had, and how nervous he was about the fight. All he could talk about was his fear of getting his leg busted up with low kicks, his body with the knee strikes, and his head with elbows. The most amazing thing to me was that here was a fighter with superior talent, an undefeated record, and some of the strongest punches and kicks I had ever seen. The challenge for me as a trainer was to get my fighter to concentrate on his own strengths and not on his opponent's. If I could get him to fight his fight, he would win.

I began by exploring his strengths one by one, and convincing him that even though his opponent had great leg kicks, and good elbows and knees, my fighter's strengths were still greater. I further instilled in him that if he imposed his will on his opponent, then his opponent would have to fight by my fighter's rules, and the knees, elbows, and leg kicks would be irrelevant. As the fight began, I convinced my fighter that he should fight as he always had, and not try to change who and what he was, simply because the rules were different. During the first two rounds, my fighter fought brilliantly, only allowing a few knees and leg kicks to land. In the third and final round, the strangest thing happened. My fighter hurt his opponent with a three-punch combination. As this happened, he looked towards me with a half-smile, then finished his opponent with two front knees to the mid-section.

Just as in social situations it is true in the fight game too. Just be yourself. It requires less energy and you will show your best. Plus, you'll make it look easy.

> Next time you fight, you're going to win because you are ready. Because the power is there, because the wind is there, and because the attitude is there. And I'm going to stand in your corner and watch you eat your opponent alive and spit out the bones. Now wasn't that a visual that would make your opponent cringe.

Parker Shelton scores with a completely spontaneous move right on the nose of Jeff Smith
(From the archives of Pro-Action Publishing)

Kinetic Energy Quiz

1. Explain how speed can outweigh the benefits of mass.

It takes a lot of energy to set a massive object into motion. When you expend energy, you get tired. A light-weight fighter can therefore be quicker than a heavyweight, without sacrificing as much energy. Twice the speed increases the kinetic energy by the square.

2. Why is kinetic energy capable of doing so much damage?

A strike that is thrown twice as fast as your opponent's strike, will have twice the impulse, and twice the ability to move your opponent back. But it will have four times the kinetic energy, and will penetrate four times as far, and do four times the damage. In the kinetic energy equation, the speed is squared. Mass only provides wallop (the ability to knock something over). Kinetic energy does damage.

3. Why is it beneficial to use a striking weapon that employs a surface area that is as small as possible?

Penetrating force is produced best when the force is focused over an area as small as possible, because the force per square inch will be greater. This can be demonstrated using a board and your bed at home. First place a large wooden board on top of your mattress. Then climb up on the bed and stand on top of the board. Even though the mattress is soft, you will notice hardly any indentation at all from the weight of your body. Now, remove the board and climb up on the bed again. Stand on one foot only. Is there greater penetration when your weight is spread over the smaller area of your foot only, than when it is spread over the whole area of the wooden board?

4. What are the advantages/disadvantages of gaining weight before an upcoming fight?

If you're fighting in weight classes, it might be to your advantage to be at the top of your weight class. A few extra pounds will give you the ability to move your opponent backward, especially when he is tired. If there is no weight class however, and the range in weight of the people you will be fighting is great, it may be to your advantage not to gain too much weight, because the extra weight makes you slower, and a lighter fighter will have the advantage kinetic energy-wise.

5. What effect does "imposing your will" have on an opponent?

The mind is a very powerful tool. Having confidence and a belief in yourself will often give you more respect than perhaps you are worthy of. An opponent who has superb technical skill and experience may lose a fight before it has even begun, simply because your confidence strips him of his own.

6. Is it possible to get knocked out by your opponent's strike, even if you are imposing your will on him?

Of course! If your opponent's strike is powerful enough. Just having confidence and "thinking" that you are not going to get knocked out will not be enough. But confidence sure helps!

Glossary

Acceleration–Changes in speed and/or direction. An object that is in motion and changes its direction (a car driving up the clover leaf on-ramp to the highway), will accelerate even if there is no change in speed. You can feel that acceleration is taking place by the way your body lurches forward, back, or sideways.

Center Of Gravity–The point on an object where all its weight seems to be focused. On an object of uniform shape and weight, the center of gravity is in the middle. On an object of non-uniform shape and weight, the center of gravity is toward the heavier end. To remain stable, the center of gravity should be as low as possible, and above the foundation.

Energy–That which enables you to do work. If you have a lot of energy, you can do a lot of work.

F=ma–The force is equal to the mass times the acceleration. The more massive a fighter, and the more he can accelerate, the more force he can produce.

Impulse–Change in momentum, or the force times the time interval. The shorter the time, the greater the force, and vice versa.

Inertia–Resistance to change in motion. An object at rest tends to stay at rest; an object in motion tends to stay in motion.

Kinetic Energy–Half the mass times the speed squared. Kinetic energy depends on the mass and the speed of the object. If a fighter can double his speed, he can quadruple his kinetic energy. Kinetic energy has a great capability of doing damage.

Mass–The quantity of matter in an object. When acted upon by gravity, we can use mass interchangeably with weight.

Momentum–The product of the mass of an object and its velocity. The heavier the object, and the faster it travels, the greater the momentum.

Pounds Per Square Inch–The narrower the base of an object, the more pounds per square inch. A narrow base will be less stable than a wide base, but it will also have more penetrating capability.

Resonance–A vibrating force or wave that causes a vibration in an object at its natural vibration frequency.

Squared-A number multiplied by itself

Velocity-A measure of the speed of an object and its direction

CHAPTER 8
Physics And Strategy

P hysics applies to all people at all times; you can't get away from it. Furthermore, it can work either for you or against you. It is now time to rise to a new level and learn how to apply the principles of physics on sparring. Without specifying a particular art, this section is intended to compare stand-up type fights (karate, kick-boxing) and ground fights (grappling), and show how the concepts of physics and strategy apply to both.

Before you can gain proficiency as a fighter, you must learn proper mechanics of technique. This is called the mechanical stage of learning, or learning "by rote". Simply put, it is memorization without understanding. The mechanical stage will do you little good in actual sparring, yet it is needed to provide a foundation for continued growth.

The second stage of learning is called understanding. When you have reached this level, you will know why you do a particular technique and when, and why you do the moves in a particular sequence. You can now answer questions about the technique, but without necessarily being proficient in its execution.

The third stage of learning is called application. This is where you can actually use what you have learned in an unrehearsed sparring match.

The fourth stage of learning is called correlation. Correlation means that you can see how the concepts that you have learned for one technique can be applied to another, or how the concepts you have learned for stand-up fighting can be applied to grappling, and vice versa. Few martial artists achieve this highest level, and few instructors teach it. If you are one of the lucky few, you can now
diversify in the martial arts without spending years perfecting a particular art. Providing that you have learned sound mechanics of technique for each art, at this stage your knowledge from one art will carry over to another. This is when you can become your own instructor.

This section is about concepts rather than techniques. If you understand the concepts, there won't be a need to learn specific techniques for every conceivable situation. If you understand the concepts, you can fight anybody anywhere.

Ten Fundamental Fighting Concepts

The following concepts are not necessarily listed in their order of importance, nor are they the only important concepts in a fight. I have included an example of a specific technique for each concept. We will then discuss each concept in more detail. For the purpose of this section, it is also assumed that both you and your opponent fight empty handed, and that you fight one person at a time only.

1. **Use stronger tools against weaker tools.** In a stand-up fight, use your elbow to block your opponent's round house kick. In a ground fight, use your leg to break a wrist grab.

2 **Use techniques that can be escalated.** In a stand-up fight, finishing strikes should follow set-up strikes. In a ground fight, a joint lock can be escalated to a dislocation technique, which can be escalated to a breaking technique.

3. **Eliminate several of your opponent's weapons simultaneously.** In a stand-up fight, attack when your opponent is at a disadvantaged position; when he is on one leg and is unable to move away. In a ground fight, apply a joint lock while simultaneously pressing out your opponent's head.

4. **Use your sense of touch.** In a stand-up fight, when shoulder to shoulder with your opponent, any small move will be telegraphed through feel. In a ground fight, train with a blind fold to enhance your sense of touch.

5. **Use several weapons together.** In a stand-up fight, throw combinations. In a ground fight, lock your opponent's legs with your legs and execute a figure four choke.

6. **Use shock value to split your opponent's focus.** In a stand-up fight, look for signs of weakness, and attack the same target multiple times. In a ground fight, grab soft tissue areas where sensitive nerves are located.

7. **Rely on superior defense.** In a stand-up fight, combine defense with offense. In a ground fight, continuously look for weakness.

8. **Rely on speed and surprise,** and the "DON'T WAIT–CREATE" principle. Be in charge. In a stand-up fight, initiate the attack. In a ground fight, be explosive.

9. **The inferior position is not necessarily a weakness.** In a stand-up fight, use strategy to reverse positions when cornered. In a ground fight, take advantage of your opponent's higher center of gravity when on your back.

10. **Use logical sequencing of techniques.** In general, logical techniques are those that have a smooth flow with no awkward movements. Logic also involves distance and positioning.

Use Stronger Tools Against Weaker Tools

Strength is a combination of the anatomical composition of your weapon and correct strategy (distance, timing, movement, etc). The elbow, for example, is a strong weapon because it is rather small and hard, and can be used to inflict a considerable amount of pain against the bony areas of your opponent's shins, insteps, or jaw line. According to physics, because of the small surface area of the elbow, it allows you to use more pounds per square inch than if you use the whole surface area of your hand. Because of the close proximity of the elbow to the body, you can rely on your body mass to generate power. You do this by keeping your elbow in front of your body and letting the movement of your strike originate in your body. Strategically, because the elbow is closer to your body than the hand, you can protect your mid-section with your elbow and arm, while simultaneously using the elbow as a "striking block". By blocking your opponent's kick with your elbow, offense and defense is accomplished simultaneously. When blocking a kick with your elbow, your opponent will experience a great deal of pain, which will make him fearful of throwing that kick again. You have therefore eliminated one of his effective weapons.

Note: Remember that the concept we are working is not how to use your elbow against your opponent's shin, but rather how to use a stronger weapon against a weaker weapon. The elbow is merely an example. What other types of strong against weak techniques can you think of?

Here, Benny "The Jet" Urquidez uses his stronger knife edge side thrust kick against his opponent's weaker knee.
[From the archives of Pro-Action Publishing]

Because concepts apply to all martial arts, if your goal is to reach the highest level of learning; that of correlation, you must be able to apply the same concepts that you use for a stand-up fight to a ground fight. As long as you have a basic understanding of ground work and the anatomical limitations of the joints, this is true even if you have never studied jiu-jitsu in particular. To apply the concept of strong against weak in grappling, you will not try to find ways to use your elbow against your opponent's shin or any other area, as this would be technique oriented. Rather, you will find ways to use your strength against your opponent's weakness. According to physics, in a ground fight your strength usually comes through leverage (torque) and the understanding that a grip will break at its weakest point. When your opponent grabs your wrist, you can break the grip by concentrating your efforts against where your opponent's fingers meet rather than against the back of his hand. In what other ways can you use strong against weak?

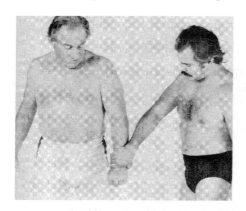  

In grappling, you can also use strong against weak by reinforcing your grip. Note how Gene LeBell's opponent grabs him in a single wrist grab. To defend against this, Gene LeBell reinforces the grip with his own free hand and forearm and drops his opponent to his knees.
(From the archives of Pro-Action Publishing)

Here, Gene LeBell uses his stronger arm against his opponent's weaker chin.
(From the archives of Pro-Action Publishing)

Use Techniques That Can Be Escalated

Escalation, in fighting, means to increase the intensity. In a stand-up fight, the last technique should feel worse than the previous technique. According to physics, this can be done by throwing combinations that have a natural flow, in which the speed can continuously build throughout the combination. Natural flow means less start/stop movement and less need to overcome inertia. The higher speed of the last strike translates into power. Strategically, escalation of power is intended to end the fight. First, by striking the same target harder and harder, the anatomical limitation of that target will eventually give in to the force. Second, by striking multiple targets harder and harder, your opponent will feel overwhelmed and be unable to defend against the strikes. Striking multiple targets is likely to create openings on the knock-out target.

In a stand-up fight, force can also be escalated by going from a block, to a strike, to a joint lock, as demonstrated by Benny "The Jet" Urquidez.
(From the archives of Pro-Action Publishing)

Again, the concept we are working is not to build speed through combinations, but to escalate the force, regardless of what type of techniques you use. In sports grappling, a technique should be escalated to the point of submission. First, gain a joint lock and apply pressure just enough to cause pain. If your opponent has a high threshold for pain, or if he is stubborn and continues to resist, escalate the technique into a possible dislocation of the joint (by now the referee should have stepped in). The next stage is the actual breaking of the joint. According to physics, a technique can be escalated by going against the natural movement of the joint. Doing damage takes relatively little force, both because of the anatomical limitations of the joint and because of torque, especially if the lever arm is long. Strategically, escalation of force is used to get pain compliance. At the earliest stage, there is no permanent damage done to the joint, and as soon as the grip is released, the pain will go away. But, knowing that a dislocation or break is imminent, is often enough to make a person submit.

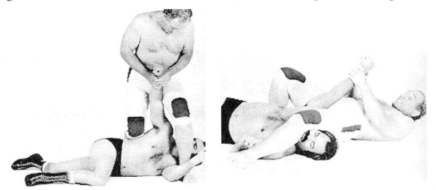

Force can also be escalated by going from a knee press with control of the arm to a full arm bar, as demonstrated by Gene LeBell.
(From the archives of Pro-Action Publishing)

Note: In a high threat street encounter, you may skip the intermediate dislocation stage and go into breaking right away.

Eliminate Several Of Your Opponent's Weapons Simultaneously

When your opponent uses a weapon, it is momentarily tied up in that technique. In a stand-up fight, when your opponent throws a punch, he is unable to simultaneously cover his ribs on the side of the punching arm. This gives you an automatic opening. In a ground fight, when your opponent grabs you with both hands, he is unable to simultaneously strike you. Providing that it is not your wrists that he is grabbing, this leaves your hands free for striking or grabbing.

The fewer effective weapons your opponent has, the less diverse he will be, and the less you will have to worry about. In a stand-up fight, you can rely on the "completion of motion" principle, which states that before another technique can be initiated, the motion of the first technique must first complete itself. This is especially beneficial whenever your opponent throws a kick, but can be used with punches as well. First, when your opponent kicks, the kicking leg will be tied up in the technique until the kick is complete. You will therefore know where that weapon is. In addition, because the legs are used for walking, your opponent won't be able to reposition himself until the motion of the kick is complete. This gives you a strategical advantage. In essence, you are tying up not only your opponent's kick (which he is using at the moment), but also his hands. Think about this: how beneficial is it to throw punches simultaneous with kicks? They won't be very powerful, because your body must have the opportunity to reset into its stance before initiating the second technique.

According to physics, when your opponent kicks, you can rely on his narrow foundation to unbalance him with a counter-attack, which will make it even more difficult for him to use another weapon against you simultaneously. The principle is not to attack when your opponent is on one leg, but to eliminate the use of several weapons. This can also be done through positioning. By working from an angle to the side, you can eliminate many of your opponent's techniques. By positioning yourself behind your opponent, you can eliminate most of his techniques.

Which weapons are being eliminated simultaneously in this sparring match between Hayes and Bob Engle? Answer: both the kick and the punches; the kick because of the leg check, and the punches because the fighter is forced backward and taken by surprise.
[From the archives of Pro-Action Publishing, photo by Joe Griffith]

In a ground fight, several weapons can be eliminated simultaneously by pressing out your opponent's head. The neck is an inherently weak area of our anatomy, and therefore relatively easy to control. When your opponent is on his back or stomach, if you turn his head to the side and place your shin across his jaw line, it will be extremely difficult for him to move or apply any type of effective technique against you. It can therefore be said that the person who controls the head, controls the fight. Applying a joint lock in a chaotic situation can be rather difficult, because it requires the use of fine motor skills. But once you have control of the head, you can take your time to properly apply a joint lock. Once you have control of the head, you can even ask your opponent to position his hands for you: "Place your left hand against the small of your back! Turn it palm up! Don't move!" Increase the pressure on his head until he complies. Because both your hands are free, and because you have compliance, you can now use fine motor skills to apply the joint lock correctly.

According to physics, you are eliminating several of your opponent's weapons by using the pounds per square inch principle (your shin against your opponent's jaw line). What is not as obvious is that you are also using leverage against your opponent's head. Because his head is unable to turn a full 360 degrees, once it gets to its maximum turn, very little force is required to produce a high torque. Impulse is also increased because the neck has very little give. Your opponent is therefore controlled rather easily. Strategically, you are a relying on not only pain compliance, but also the anatomical limitations of the neck.

Which weapons are being eliminated simultaneously by Gene LeBell? Answer: the left leg because of the ankle lock, and both arms because of positioning.
(From the archives of Pro-Action Publishing)

Use Your Sense Of Touch

Most people rely almost exclusively on sight, and without it we feel extremely limited. But your sense of touch should compliment your sight. Furthermore, there are times when you will have to rely on touch exclusively. You should therefore take time to develop this important sense. In a stand-up fight, the most obvious time you can use touch is in close quarters, when you are shoulder to shoulder with your opponent, generally in a clinch. If you feel movement on the left side of your body, he will most likely throw a strike with his right hand. This is because the movement of a strike originates in the body. If he is pressing against you, you can set him up by first pressing back, and then quickly take a subtle step to the side and counter-strike. He will now lose balance and fall forward and into your technique. According to physics, you are using your opponent's momentum against himself. When he falls forward and into your strike, you are adding the momentum of your strike to his forward movement, with the result of an increase in power. Strategically, by relying on touch, you will know what type of technique that is coming, and can therefore prepare your defense and counter in advance. Surprising your opponent with a strike when he is off balance will also shock him and affect him mentally.

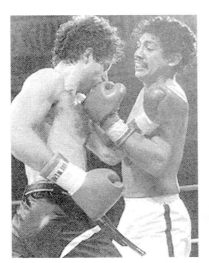

As shown by Dan Magnus and Babe Gallegos, when working at very close range, you can often feel any small move in your opponent's body and strike the moment he creates a gap.
(From the archives of Pro-Action Publishing, phot by James Baka)

Because of the close proximity to your opponent in a grappling situation, there will be many times when your eyesight will be limited. By relying on your sense of touch, you will still be successful at finding and working a variety of joint locks. I recommend training blind folded every now and then. This is easier done in grappling than in stand-up fighting, because it is assumed that you will be in contact with your opponent the whole time. When you can control your opponent without actually seeing what you are doing, you will heighten your awareness of what is going on.

Both fighters are very close and have their heads turned in opposite directions. Who wins this match may be determined by who is able to control his opponent through feel.
(From the archives of Pro-Action Publishing)

According to physics in grappling, your sense of touch will be applied mostly through leverage. Presses are a little more difficult, because they require precision against a small target (jaw line, pressure point on arm, etc), which may be difficult to find without sight. Strategically, touch allows you many opportunities. If your opponent blind folds you, you are still not helpless. When your opponent is behind you, you will still know where his weapons are.

Use Several Weapons Together

Using several weapons together is not the same as throwing a kick and a punch at the same time, as discussed above. When using several weapons together, you still need to ensure that you have full control of balance and that you can utilize your body mechanics to obtain maximum power. In a stand-up fight, this can be accomplished by throwing your strikes in combinations. According to physics, using singular strikes take a lot of effort, because you must overcome inertia with each strike. Combinations allow you to build speed continuously throughout, providing that your combinations are logical, which will be discussed later. Strategically, combinations allow you to overwhelm your opponent. Because it is not possible to block all targets at the same time, this provides you with many open targets.

Combinations allow you to preserve your momentum and overwhelm your opponent, until you can land a good finishing blow, as shown by Benny "The Jet" Urquidez.
(From the archives of Pro-Action Publishing)

In a ground fight, it is a little easier to use several weapons at exactly the same time without losing balance or power. For example, with your opponent in the prone position (on his stomach) with you on his back, lock your opponent's legs with your legs and execute a rear figure four choke. You will now spread your weight over your opponent, which according to physics makes you very stable, and it will be difficult for him to throw you off. Strategically, because he will be experiencing pain and defeat at two different places simultaneously, his mind and body focus will split.

Here, Gene LeBell uses his leg to lock his opponent's leg, while simultaneously applying a lock to his opponent's arm, and pressure on his neck
(From the archives of Pro-Action Publishing)

Use Shock Value To Split Your Opponent's Focus

The purpose of shock value is not to knock your opponent out or to choke him out, but to get a reaction or to instill fear. In a stand-up fight this can be accomplished by attacking a vulnerable target repeated times. The nerves on the outside portion of your opponent's thigh is such a target. By flicking a quick round house kick against your opponent's thigh, he will soon become protective of this leg and reluctant to place it within reach. In physics, shock value has very little application, with the strategic advantage being the most valuable.

Muay Thai fighters know the value of a well placed thigh kick.
(From the archives of Pro-Action Publishing)

Some grappling matches last in excess of thirty minutes, where neither fighter is moving very much. But inactivity doesn't win a fight if that inactivity doesn't cause pain or exhaustion as in a time hold. If you are the lighter fighter, you are likely to find yourself on your back with your opponent on top of you. Because of his weight, you will expend much energy trying to get him off you but without accomplishing much. Strategically, you can use shock value to get an immediate reaction which will momentarily split your opponent's focus and enable you to break free. By grabbing soft tissue areas i.e., love handles, inside thighs, inside upper arms you will create an immediate reaction through pain, even though it will have no lasting effect. You must now take advantage of this reaction and move to a better position.

If you were in the disadvantaged position, and you had access to your opponent's face, this type of grab would have a most shocking effect.
(From the archives of Pro-Action Publishing)

Rely On Superior Defense

It has been said that, "the best defense is offense", and it is true. However, I would like to take that a step further and say that if you can make your offensive move and your defensive move the same, you will consistently be one step ahead of your opponent. Part of this was demonstrated in the first example on using your elbow to block your opponent's kick. In a stand-up fight, you should also look at using movement and position in combination with offense. For example, side-stepping a punch and simultaneously throwing a round house kick will not only accomplish defense, but will also have the effect of your opponent walking into your kick. According to physics, this uses the principles of mass and momentum. Strategically, you are cutting the time it takes to accomplish your goal. Benny "The Jet" calls the competive match in the ring, "physical chess."

Benny "The Jet" side-steps a punch, placing himself in a superior position to the outside, from where he can counter with a palm strike to the head.
(From the archives of Pro-Action Publishing)

Superior defense in grappling also relies on offense. We have already talked about how a grapplingmatch often goes into a stalemate, where not much seems to happen. It is possible for a small person to keep a bigger opponent from taking him to submission just by covering up all vulnerable targets; by no presenting your opponent with fingers or wrists, and by not exposing your neck. However, this will only win the fight if your opponent tires much faster than you and is unable to keep the pressure on. In order to reverse the superiority of the fight, you must consistently look for weaknesses in your opponent's defense. Focus away from the area of attack. If he is trying to choke you, instead of grabbing his arms or hands to prevent the choke, try to grab his chin to get control of his head. Remember, the fighter who controls the head, controls the fight. By grabbing the chin, you can raise your opponent's center of gravity and destroy his balance. Strategically, this works because your opponent's focus will be on his attack; on choking you, and not on defending against a counter-attack to his head.

Before your opponent can mount an effective attack, use a defensive throw to unbalance him.
(From the archives of Pro-Action Publishing)

Rely on Speed And Surprise

It is usually better to act than to react. This is because whoever initiates action also determines the pace and the course of the fight. The person who acts will be the leader. In a stand-up fight, this means that you must consistently be a step faster than your opponent. He will now be forced to defend against your techniques, rather than you defending against his. Also be explosive. Work with different speeds to create surprise reactions in your opponent. Explosiveness comes from rapid acceleration in a short distance. The faster your initial move, the more explosive your technique.

Explosiveness is also reflected in how you carry yourself. Is Benny "The Jet" ready to attack?
(From the archives of Pro-Action Publishing)

On the ground, you can use explosiveness to reverse positions, or to keep your opponent from gaining a control hold. If you are in the supine position (on your back) with your opponent straddling you, before he has lowered his center of gravity and become stable, raise your hips explosively and without warning in an attempt to throw him off. It is now imperative that you don't stop there, but continue using explosiveness to get up on your knees and reverse positions. The problem with working with one speed only is that your opponent will feel any movement in your body and counteract it. Even though you may be the one initiating the move, because you give your opponent "prior warning" he can apply effective defense.

When held down, your next technique must happen with speed and surprise.
(From the archives of Pro-Action Publishing)

The Inferior Position Is Not Necessarily A Weakness

Some positions are less desirable than others because they are difficult to fight from, and because they mentally give a feeling of inferiority. In a stand-up fight, the inferior position is usually with your back against a wall or the ropes of the ring. But by being aware of your position, you can use strategy to reverse it. When you get within one foot of the ropes, start side-stepping the attack. Or if your opponent is pushing you back with his shoulder, start circling with your back away from the wall or ropes and toward the center of the ring. A natural tendency is to automatically mirror your opponent's moves. This can be used strategically to circle your opponent into the inferior position on the ropes. According to physics, you are using the principle of non-resistance, and of allowing the momentum to continue. This takes less effort than if you were to pressure back in a straight line. What appears to be the inferior position can now be reversed and turned into the superior position.

When in the inferior position against the ropes, Benny "The Jet" uses movement to avoid the attack, allowing his opponent's momentum to continue in a straight line.
(From the archives of Pro-Action Publishing)

In grappling, using locks against the joints is common practice. For example, the wrist lock can be applied both in an outside motion (away from your centerline) and inside motion (toward your centerline). The drawback of a wrist lock is that it requires fine motor skills to apply. It is therefore not practical in a chaotic situation. A wrist lock should usually follow, rather than precede, some other controlling technique, like a forearm press to your opponent's head. If you attempt a wrist lock without controlling the rest of your opponent's body, he may try to wrestle out of it. By learning how to transition from one wrist lock to another, you can again use the law of non-resistance. When your opponent attempts to wrestle out of a wrist lock, he is likely to try going against the direction of the technique. If you have your opponent in an outside wrist lock, and providing that the wrist lock is not yet fully applied, he can get out of it by rotating his arm to the inside (toward the centerline). But this also allows you to transition to the inside wrist lock. In effect, if you let your opponent, he will position himself in the inside wrist lock for you. Strategically, he will have accomplished nothing; you still have him in a wrist lock.

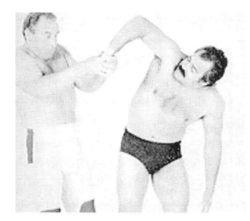

When Gene LeBell's opponent raises his arm in an attempt to break the wrist grab, Gene LeBell goes with the motion underneath the arm and transitions smoothly into another joint lock.
(From the archives of Pro-Action Publishing)

Use Logical Sequencing Of Techniques

As we have already discussed, there are many strategical benefits that can be attained by working your techniques in combinations rather than focusing on single strikes. This section will deal with logical sequencing of your techniques. In stand-up fighting, a jab will logically not follow an uppercut in close quarters. Why? First, the uppercut is a short range technique, while the jab is a long range technique. According to physics, if the jab is thrown from close range, it will be smothered because you are using the "wrong" distance for the technique. You will be unable to build momentum for power. Strategically, the jab is not a finishing strike, but a set-up strike, and should therefore precede a power technique, such as the uppercut. If your opponent moves back and creates distance, it would be better to follow with a rear cross or an overhand strike (which are both finishing punches), rather than a jab.

The bottom line is that if your techniques are logical, they will be thrown with less effort and become much faster. And, as we have previously learned, through speed comes power. Logical sequencing of techniques will keep your fighting range optimal. It is possible to throw an uppercut following a side thrust kick, but because the side thrust kick is likely to knock your opponent back, and the uppercut is a close range technique, if you attempt this combination, you will need to utilize more and bigger movements to close distance. Aside from telegraphing your technique, this is also uneconomical.

In ground fighting, logical sequencing of techniques should also be considered. For example, if you execute a rear choke on an opponent on his stomach, it would not make sense to follow this technique with a finger lock. A better combination would be to work a series of techniques that eventually lead into the rear choke, and to finish with the choke.

Is the high side thrust kick a logical technique? Well, it depends on what happened prior to the kick. If the kick was thrown in an attempt to strike an opponent who is standing, it would be a logical technique. If the opponent was already on the ground, the kick would be highly illogical.
(From the archives of Pro-Action Publishing, photo by Raemar Video)

Indomitable Spirit

One last thing that ought to be mentioned is the martial spirit. When I was studying karate, we were told that one of the characteristics of a superior fighter is indomitable spirit. The instructor explained that this means "to have a spirit that can't be dominated". When I became an instructor myself, I did some research into the word origin and found that it stems from the word "diamond", which, in turn, means "untamed". A diamond is the hardest material we know of, and the only way to cut a diamond is with another diamond. In essence, indomitable spirit means a spirit that can't be broken.

The reason a diamond is so strong is because the molecular pattern is so complex. I once observed a board breaking demonstration where a young kid about twelve years old was going to break a one-inch board with his fist. When he struck the board, it didn't break. The young martial artist grabbed the board from the holder, took one quick look at it, and turned it one quarter of a turn. When he struck again, the board broke. This youngster knew something about the building material of the board, and where the point of strength and weakness were. If you attempt to break against the grain, it will take more force than if you try to break with the grain. Likewise, if the grain is wavy or has a knot in it, a higher force will be required to break the board. It can therefore be said that the more complex the grain (the pattern), the more force will be required to break it.

Because of the complex molecular structure of the diamond, you wouldn't dream of trying to break one with your fist. Much of the value of the diamond is also derived from it being "multi-faceted". In martial arts, you can be multi-faceted by cross training in different arts. On a grander martial scale, this can be applied to whole armies. The general who leads an army of a thousand men, whose only quality is muscular strength, will soon be defeated by the opposing army who has a mixture of men with qualitites such as strength, speed, intelligence, etc.

"The brave can fight, the careful can guard, the intelligent can communicate."

- Sun Tzu, The Art Of War

The more you can diversify your skill, the more likely you are to succeed in battle. I am not implying that you should be a "jack of all trades", but that you should educate yourself on how to use your skill in many different situations. If all you know is how to strike and kick, and you end up on the ground, the battle may well be over. The opposite is also true. Today, when cross training is so popular, we see a lot of grapplers studying Muay Thai and kick-boxing, and vice versa. In a nut-shell: don't place all your eggs in one basket ... and hide an ace in your back pocket.

Conclusion

Throughout my years of study in the martial arts, I think that perhaps what has intrigued me the most are the many contradictions. In modern day language, martial arts means the intricate study of combat. Because combat means battle, struggle, conflict, it seems logical to think of a martial artist as a person who has studied conflict and who is skilled at combat. The more traditional way of interpreting the term martial arts is through budo, which means "the way of the warrior". Aikido founder and master Morihei Ueshiba emphasized that "a martial art must be a procreative force, producing love, which in turn will lead to a creative, rich life" (The Spirit Of Aikido–by Kisshomaru Ueshiba, Kodansha International). Most martial arts instructors drill into us from the beginning that we are only to use the arts when we absolutely have to. And the philosophy of the arts is often those of both love and war.

When looking at power and the principles of physics, I have found a great many paradoxes as well. For instance, the gain/lose situations I have been mentioning throughout the book. You sometimes will need to give something up in order to gain a greater advantage. For example:

- When pinning your opponent to the ground, you will be more stable, and it will be more difficult for him to throw you off, if you spread your weight as much as possible. On the other hand, when you use only a very small part of your body when pinning (the elbow or knee, for example) will make you less stable. Yet it enables you to increase the intensity of your technique by placing more pounds per square inch on the target.

- It is better to be heavy than to be light, because more mass means more force behind your strikes. But more mass also means more inertia, more difficult to set in motion. Without motion, there is no power.

When working with the martial arts, you must tilt the law of averages (the probability) to your advantage. When rolling a die for example, what is the probability that you will roll a six? Because there are six sides to the die, the probability is one in 6. That means that if you were to roll the die 6 times, you are likely to roll a 6 one of those times. If you roll the die twenty-four times, you are likely to roll a 6 four of those times. In pure probability, as in the case with the die, not much can be done to affect the law of averages. But what if you were to take a multiple choice test, with four possible answers to each question? If such a test was taken blind folded, the probability that you would score correctly would be one in four. Without any knowledge whatsoever of the questions being asked, you would still come through the test with a score of 25%. If you needed a score of 75% to pass this test, you had only to increase your knowledge by 50% and not by 75%, as one might have thought before taking the test.

Before any action at all is taken, you should look at the probability of a successful outcome. Because of their athletic build, speed, and flexibility, some people appear to be "naturals". The person who is not a "natural" can still come out on top by evaluating his situation beforehand, and then use opposing qualities to exploit his opponent's strengths.

During The Ultimate Fighting Championship I in the 1990s, Sumo wrestler Teila Tuli (410 lbs.) met Savate fighter Gerard Gordeau (216 lbs.). About twenty seconds into the fight, Teila charged forward. While back-pedaling, Gerard threw several punches to Teila's head that did little or no damage. It was obvious that the almost twice as heavy Teila had the momentum and power advantage. Shortly thereafter however, Teila lost his balance and went down. Although he had several seconds to get back to his feet, the inertia of 410 pounds of weight was too much to get up in time. This is a fine example of how the advantage of weight can be exploited by a lighter opponent. The heavier a fighter, the more momentum he can produce, but the more energy he will have to expend.

A more graphic example, in order to prove the point, is the following. For those that enjoy their martial arts history comes this classic anecdote of the first paid event for Benny Urquidez, a year before he became known as "The Jet".

Dateline 1975, Honolulu, Hawaii. The event, The World Series of Martial Arts. A true tough-man contest that was a 20 year precursor to the UFC mentioned on the previous page. This was a two-day event which boasted all types of fighters, from martial artists to barroom brawlers. There was no safety equipment, no time limit and no rules. The only attraction for the competitors was a $5,000.00 cash prize. At the end of the second day, we witnessed a 230 pound 6'1" Dana Goodson facing a 5'6", 130 pound Benny Urquidez.

Urquidez, long known for being cool under pressure and an excellent strategist related the following story to Stuart Sobel, the publisher of Pro-Action Publishing, who in turn related the events of the day to me.

"I knew I couldn't out-muscle Dana, he was just too big. My strategy", Urquidez confided, "would be to do something he would never expect. I would attack him, not just run from him like his other opponents. But not just attack, I planned to attack him like a mad-man. The bell sounded. I stayed out of his way initially. When I saw my opening I rushed him. I slipped his jab and grabbed him around the neck in a clench. My feet were dangling off the ground. I kept kneeing him on his body and hitting him in the face with my free hand and elbow. Dana was becoming quite frustrated with me because he had no distance to hit or kick. He kept trying to brush me off, but I was not going to let go. I was like a leech, sucking on his blood. Finally he toppled over. As soon as he hit the ground I jumped on top, covering his upper body by spreading out as wide as I could. He tried to bump me off, so I spit out my mouthpiece and bit him on the chest. I was able to pin him for the count of three, which is all it took to win. He was a good sport. We shook hands after it was over."

Benny "The Jet" became the extreme inside fighter. He closed the range on his much larger opponent and gave him no distance to strike. Next, he raised Dana's center of gravity by making his upper body suddenly weighing an additional 130 pounds.

He created a barrage of kinetic energy. The strikes and knees to the body were being forced in a direction perpendicular to the base. This was all supported on a small base line, his feet. Dana naturally would become unstable. Without any outside support he had to fall. Finally, Urquidez spread his weight out over the supine Goodson to make it difficult to throw him off by keeping his center of gravity low as possible. When Dana tried to use explosive power to bump his 100 pound lighter opponent, "The Jet" bit him for a pain diversion. That gave him the time he needed for the referee's three-count. Truly classic strategy, and a wonderful use of the laws of physics.

What makes physics so appealing is that it is not really up for debate. The principles of physics have been established through the scientific method, where scientists recognize problems, form a hypothesis (an educated guess), and perform experiments to test the hypothesis. Once the outcome is established, a theory is formed. When a hypothesis has been tested over and over without being contradicted, it may become known as a law or principle.

The principles of physics apply to all people at all times, regardless of which art you study. Understanding physics therefore allows you to understand power, speed, and endurance as a whole, and then to work these principles to your benefit. Size and weight for example, may seem like an advantage, but it is also a limitation. Whether the glass is half-full or half-empty depends on what's in the glass and how thirsty you are. It is my hope that this book will help you use physics to make your strengths stronger and make your limitations shrink to nothing.

" I can move the whole earth, if I can stand on a platform with a lever in my hand."
-Archimedes

"Strategy is the craft of the warrior"
-Miyamoto Musashi, A Book Of Five Rings

Good Luck!
Never Quit!
Never Give Up!
Never Say Die!

Classic Titles From PRO-ACTION PUBLISHING